Come Out and Win

Other books in the Queer Action/Queer Ideas series

Out Law: What LGBT Youth Should Know about Their Legal Rights, by Lisa Keen

Come Out and Win

Organizing Yourself,

Your Community,

and Your World

Sue Hyde

Queer Action/Queer Ideas,
a series edited by Michael Bronski

Beacon Press, Boston

BEACON PRESS
25 Beacon Street
Boston, Massachusetts 02108-2892
www.beacon.org

Beacon Press books
are published under the auspices of
the Unitarian Universalist Association of Congregations.

10 09 08 07   8 7 6 5 4 3 2 1

This book is printed on acid-free paper that meets the uncoated paper
ANSI/NISO specifications for permanence as revised in 1992.

Composition by Wilsted & Taylor Publishing Services

Library of Congress Control Number: 2007924181

For Jade, Jesse, and Max,
who shape, structure, and fill my days and nights
with significance, meaning, and love.

Contents

A Note from the Series Editor

Political organizing is a cross between an art, a science, and an instinct. Like art or science, it is not a social frivolity or the work of dilettantes. It is as much a social necessity as food and shelter. As citizens of this country and of the world, we are mandated to improve not only our own lot, but that of our friends, comrades, and neighbors as well.

This book, by the consummate organizer and activist Sue Hyde, is a primer for how to change the world in which we live. Her examples here—and her work in the world—are drawn from her efforts in the lesbian, gay, bisexual, and transgender communities. But the information she presents here can be used by anyone working for political and social justice.

It is extraordinary that for all of the political organizing that has been done in the LGBT community for the past half-century, no one had collected and compiled a basic how-to book of LGBT grassroots organizing. We, and Beacon Press, are proud to be able to do this now. Sue Hyde can teach us both the science and the art involved in LGBT organizing. She cannot teach us to have the instinct. Thankfully, most people in the LGBT community understand the need to make the world a better place for everyone—they have the instinct for social justice, and Hyde's book will help them act on that instinct and change the world.

MICHAEL BRONSKI
Series Editor

Foreword: Forward!

*There are many ways to contribute to social change, but there
is a difference between grassroots organizing and writing a book.
There is a difference between being an organizer and being a city
councilor. I want to be a voice affirming the value and heroism
of long-term commitment to democratic processes of community
organizing. We may hate the endless meetings, be sick of licking
envelopes, feel frustrated working across different identities and
political visions, and be drained by community cannibalism, but
we've got to continue doing the work... social change cannot
happen without old-time grassroots community organizing.*

Eric Rofes, excerpt from remarks made at the Second
Annual Summit to Resist Attacks on Gay Men's Sexual
Civil Liberties, Pittsburgh, November 13, 1998

The political movement for lesbian, gay, bisexual, and transgender
(LGBT) freedom and social justice, barely over fifty years old and a relative newcomer to national politics, has already changed the world in
which we live. We have instigated legal and policy reforms, historic
court rulings, institutional recognitions of our needs and lives, and a
national and public dialogue about our relationships and our civil
rights. We have made possible the coming out of LGBT people at both
younger ages and in higher places in the power structures of government, corporations, and religious bodies. News outlets cover LGBT
people and issues nearly every day, both our victories and our defeats.
Still, there is much more organizing and community building to do if
we are to reach our goal of ending widespread oppression of homosexuality and gender variance.

I liken political organizing to parenting: tedious, repetitive, endlessly consuming of time and energy, and yet punctuated by real break-through events and times during which we can see that the hard work has yielded positive gains. With this book, I invite you to take up the tough and rewarding tasks of organizing so that we all benefit from the pivotal political watershed moments when nothing that comes after will ever be the same. Organizing isn't glamorous or sexy and it isn't a route to wealth and fame, although if we are fortunate, we'll meet wonderful people, have opportunities for lots of great sex, and know the somewhat rich and almost famous who will want to support our work.

Organizing is simply that which is required of us to ensure that no LGBT person must ever again choose to live in silent shame in order to live at all. Let's come out and win. See you at the hustings!

1

I/You/We: The Three Pronouns of Coming Out

Coming out of the sexual-/gender-identity closet is an intensely personal experience for all who take the step. There isn't a formula, a set time, or a magically perfect way to do it. Coming out is the hard work of recognizing who we are and what we want, being honest and open with ourselves and others, and then being willing to act on that knowledge in order to live a life of integrity, wholeness, and pleasure.

The opposite of coming out of the closet is living in secrecy, fear, and shame. Staying in the closet is like living in an upended casket, dying a little bit inside every time a family member, friend, neighbor, or coworker asks what should be a friendly, innocent, and welcoming question: "Anyone special in your life?" "What did you do over the weekend?" "When will you settle down, get married, and raise a family?"

The necessary work of coming out is something that distinguishes LGBT people from all others, and yet the process is remarkably similar for all who must undertake it. It is we who consciously set ourselves apart by telling parents, family members, and closest friends that our sexual and emotional energy sparkles for someone of the same sex, or that we are attracted to both men and women, or that our birth sex does not match our internal gender identity. When we come out we identify ourselves as different from the vast majority of people we know and we distance ourselves from those who love and know us best by telling them that, in one very significant way, they knew us not at all.

Coming out of the closet is not something that all LGBT people *must* do, but imagine how many of us would be openly and identifiably LGBT if all of us did come out. It also helps put us into contact with other LGBT people. Coming out must be done repeatedly throughout our lifetimes because, unlike other minority groups who are identified by skin color or gender or other physical characteristics, LGBT people are not necessarily obvious to others. Despite popular notions of "gaydar," we wear no mark of homosexuality. Each new person we meet, each new social or employment situation we're in, summons us out of the closet. Every medical care provider, for instance, needs to know about our sexual orientation or gender identity/expression in order to provide us the best care. Every teacher of our children needs to know about our family configuration so that our kids' families are recognized and respected in the classroom. Most of us have been raised by heterosexual parents and live in a predominantly heterosexual extended family. After we come out to immediate family, we will have more opportunities to come out to grandparents, aunts, uncles, cousins, and on and on.

LGBT people report the hardships of living a closeted, secret life. With millions of words, LGBT writers and thinkers have described the toll exacted by the intimate self-censorship of the closet as blows to self-esteem and mental and physical well-being. The decision to live openly and honestly as LGBT resolves internal conflicts created when we do not tell others our personal truths, but the penalties for coming out can also be harsh. We come into closer contact with homophobia and its relentless assaults on our lives and our human dignity. Coming out of the closet vividly demonstrates to us the ways in which LGBT people are not free, not equal, and not welcome to participate in society. Paradoxically, when we come out we declare our personal existential independence from the constraints of enforced or assumed heterosexuality and bear the brunt of heterosexual supremacy and homophobia. At the precise moment we come out and slam shut a closet door behind us, the social costs of being openly lesbian, gay, bisexual, or transgender shoot up and off the charts. Suddenly, if others know we are LGBT, we can be:

- rejected by family members or friends or coworkers;
- fired from our jobs;
- denied housing or educational opportunities;

• discharged from the military;
• attacked on the street or at school;
• abandoned by our religious or other social communities;
• legally stripped of our capacity to care for our life partners and immediate family members.

Coming out carries risks but also offers rich rewards. Although it can at first seem that negotiating the world after we're out is as treacherous as negotiating the world while we're closeted, the sharp contrasts in the two experiences bear exposure.

1. We no longer live, tell, and perpetuate a lie about ourselves.
2. We are able to join the ever-growing LGBT communities in which we can build friendships, loving relationships, and long-lasting bonds with people like us who provide support, nurturance, and context for our lives.
3. We can apply ourselves to the righteous task of changing the world so that those who come after us need not endure the internal conflicts of lying, or the pain caused by external hostilities toward LGBT people.

We win the ultimate prize when we come out: to live honestly, to find community, and then to challenge homophobia as part of a historic movement for social justice for LGBT people. We win when we stand our ground and declare ourselves LGBT. We win when we enter into a community of people like ourselves. We win when we roll up our sleeves and get to work, confronting, defying, and erasing homophobia.

What Will It Take to Erase Homophobia?

Much like the old joke, "How do I get to Carnegie Hall?" "Practice, practice, practice," ridding the world of homophobia requires the concentrated work of people who are determined, thoughtful, and unwavering in the quest to erase homophobia. The LGBT social justice movement rests on the idea that each person can change his/her thinking about homosexuality because all of us who work in the movement already have changed our thinking about our own sexual or gender identities. We have lived through a change of mind and heart: our own. We have seen, felt, and acted on one fundamental change in our own lives by coming out of the closet. We have passed through three important phases of coming out:

1. I am lesbian/gay/bisexual/transgender.
2. You who share this with me are my community.
3. We will work together to change the world.

Every celebrity, elected official, musician, entertainer, athlete, doctor, union member, teacher, nurse, administrative assistant, hedge fund manager, farmer, artist, rancher, university professor, preacher, rabbi, nun, fireman, cop, actor, writer, waiter, bartender, journalist, factory worker, and child care worker who lives life openly as a lesbian, gay man, bisexual, or transgender person has experienced the same earthmoving change in their lives.

But now that we're out, what do we do? When we come face-to-face with expressions of deeply held prejudice against our selves and our communities, how can we respond in an effective, concerted, and strong-minded way? While individuals can do much in the context of their personal lives to oppose homophobia, we will be most successful—and efficient—when we join with other earnest seekers of social change. In our social movement, as is true of other social movements, the bulk of the work is accomplished by people who come together in organized groups that reinforce and weld individuals' commitments into a forceful and orderly series of actions to effect change. These organizations provide structure, strategy and tactics, leadership, and resources to LGBT people and straight allies who have the passion, the time, and the dedication to work within their communities to promote change. The LGBT social justice movement is comprised of thousands of advocacy organizations at every level of the political sphere: local, state, federal, and international. Virtually all of the LGBT advocacy organizations that are formally organized are "nonprofit" groups, by which is meant the group exists for purposes other than generating profits to shareholders. Nonprofit LGBT advocacy groups may be staffed or not or may be incorporated or not. All have members and volunteers whose time, energy, and support feed the organization. These groups are powered by ordinary people who want to create fundamental change in how lesbians, gay men, and bisexual and transgender people are thought about and treated.

New York City's famous Stonewall Rebellion of June 1969 revealed to LGBT people all across the country that by working in concert, we could fight back against government-sanctioned repression. By standing up against the routine police raids on gay bars, the dykes and fags and drag queens of Stonewall ignited our modern LGBT social movement. In 1969 there were a handful of "gay" organizations in the United States; today there are thousands of LGBT organizations and institutions to meet the interests of LGBT people in all their diversity. Community builders across the country have created groups that bring us together for wide-ranging purposes: politics, fun and recreation, emotional support, professional growth, worship, and sport. Most large and medium-size cities are home to organizations that offer social and cultural outlets, health care and mental health services, and information and support for LGBT people at every stage of life. LGBT groups cover topics such as HIV/AIDS and other health issues, education, legal and political action/advocacy, religion and spirituality, sports, recreation and fitness, youth and school-based activities, and support groups centering on coming out, starting a family, alcohol- and substance-abuse issues, domestic violence, racial identities, sexual orientations and practices, professional and employment affinities, gender variance, and HIV-positive status. Name a topic or activity of great relevance to LGBT people and it's a good bet you can find an organization that focuses on it.

The construction of LGBT community in nearly every large and medium-size city and college/university town means that most of us can find other LGBT people and meaningful LGBT community life. Social groups in our communities offer the support and camaraderie of other LGBT people to expand our own understandings of how we live as LGBT people. Political groups build the necessary structures and gather energies of committed LGBT people to take on projects of legal reform. And even for those who live in a town without a visible LGBT community, access to the Internet brings us into contact with countless other LGBT people. Most of us no longer need to live in isolation, thinking that we are the "only one." Just as the brick-and-mortar aspects of community exist for us, so, too, does the online community exist. Resources abound. Check them out. Sample what the LGBT world offers. After all, it's yours.

After we come out, though, we experience homophobia in a very different way than when we were in the closet. A closeted person experiences homophobia, and the topic of homosexuality, as something to avoid, or something that threatens to blow a cover, or even something to slyly prop up so as to deflect suspicion of queerness away from us and on to others. But once we're out, homophobia exasperates and irritates us and often motivates us by creating a different kind of internal conflict: instead of "What's wrong with me?" we think: "What's wrong with her/him/this world?" For many of us, the vexing frustrations created by homophobia call us to action.

What can we do to erase homophobia? Recognize it. Call it out. Challenge it. Defy it. Refuse to live within its stultifying confines. Work with others to wipe out homophobia from the public square and the laws and policies of public and private institutions and governments. Just as racism seems intractable in our society, homophobia seems a poison equally resistant to antidote. We must keep in mind, though, that every successful challenge to homophobia, whether personal, political, or institutional, is both a potent teaching moment and another step toward its eventual eradication.

Organizations: The Key to Action

Political organizing and action springs from LGBT groups that have social change and community organizing at the core of their missions. These groups identify and name the ways that LGBT lives are constrained by oppression of homosexuality and nontraditional gender expression. Some LGBT organizations that are not explicitly political turn their energies toward social action projects when they encounter overt homophobia. For example, school-based LGBT groups often organize to support openly LGBT students and their straight allies. But if a student group's posters are defaced with anti-LGBT graffiti and the administration fails to take strong action to support the student group by declaring a zero-tolerance policy for anti-LGBT behavior, the student organization likely will launch itself into advocacy tactics to compel the administration to take a strong stand and to galvanize other students, faculty, and staff and parents to support its cause. Of course, not all LGBT groups are or will be political groups. For instance, the (fictional) Lesbian Literary Leopards who dedicate themselves solely to a mission of holding regular book club meetings probably won't change their spots and become a roaring political machine. Move on to explore other organizations to find those that have the appetite and the gusto for political action.

Political groups or LGBT groups that can be politicized typically hunger for new and eager members. But don't charge in expecting to run the show. Remember that any organization with a history will have its own agenda or program and will want to integrate new members into the ongoing work. Be respectful. Attend at least two meetings during which your focus is as an observer; listen and learn about the group and its goals, its leadership, and its group process before you offer your opinions. After the first meeting, volunteer to take on a basic housekeeping chore for the next meeting, like bringing the lemonade or getting the handouts copied. By doing so, you express your interest and commitment without prematurely entering into policy discussions or opinion debates among members of longer standing. As you become familiar with the group and its leaders and members become familiar with you, start talking. Let your opinions and views be heard in the meetings and participate in the group's decision-making process. Assert yourself, but don't be aggressive. Collaborate and become part of the team. Your confidence will grow and others will develop confidence in you. Take advantage of opportunities to be a part of the social scene. If the group debriefs after the meeting at the local coffeehouse, join in when you can. Bring a plate of cookies to a meeting. Offer to host a potluck that precedes a meeting. Sharing food and drink brings people together in a special way that makes planning political action and sorting through a thorny issue easier and more productive.

Filling in the Organizational Gaps

If you live in a community or on a campus that is not home to an organization for LGBT people, consider getting together with a few friends to start one. Begin your discussion by brainstorming among yourselves about why a group by, for, and about LGBT people interests each of you. This will enable you to learn about all of the needs and desires you want to address. As the initiating group, you will also learn what kind of organization most interests you as a whole. If your discussion primarily centers on opportunities for social networking, outings to museums, or day trips to go hiking, then forming a social/artistic/recreational group meets those needs. If the group gets jazzed about sharing information on knitting or diving into the latest bestseller, then a hobby group meets those needs. But if your discussion returns to the problems that LGBT people experience because of homophobia and gender-expression prejudice, then there may be interest in a political action organization. This kind of organization has social change and community organizing at its core and creates durable change in the policies and laws of institutions, both public and private, working to ensure that LGBT people do not suffer arbitrary discrimination, like loss of jobs and housing or lack of access to education and health care. While informal brainstorming among friends can shed light on injustices against LGBT people, keep in mind that the group's action agenda must remain flexible and open to input from other interested people. LGBT people don't necessarily share a common experience of oppression, and new issues and new contexts for action will continually be brought forward by new members of the group.

After the initiating group has set the priority goals and formulated a draft mission of the organization, a founding meeting should be held so that interested people can join in to shape and launch the group. The initiating group must reach out to as many potentially interested people as possible so that attendance at the launch meeting is strong and a group larger than the initiators shares the crucial first phase of organization building. Methods of outreach and notification include: fliers or other forms of written announcements; postings in a local/community newspaper; and information circulated via the Net and other electronic means. But the very best way to invite folks to your launch meeting is *to talk directly and personally* with people you know, explaining why you think an LGBT organization is needed and asking them to attend the meeting and take part in the new organization's creation.

At the launch meeting, the initiating group offers an agenda that includes their vision of the new LGBT organization: its mission and goals, how it will achieve those aims, a proposed structure, and a road map or plan for the first three to six months of the group's life. Two members of the initiating group should be prepared to facilitate the discussion at the launch meeting; one or two should take notes and help the facilitators keep track of the meeting agenda and time frames for each topic. The initiating group should be prepared for attendees at the meeting to have informational questions, complementary and sometimes conflicting ideas about missions and goals, suggestions about group structure, and so on. In a room of twenty LGBT people, there can be numerous different ideas and opinions on any one subject. The facilitators must strive to allow for maximum participation by attendees while sticking to the agenda and time frames for each topic. As well, facilitators need to lead the group through a decision-making process, even if the best outcome is to postpone a final decision until the next meeting. Some attending the launch meeting will not attend a second meeting because the group's thrust and focus don't interest them; some won't come back because they don't have the time or energy to play a central role in the new organization, even though they support the formation of the group. But no attendee should leave the launch meeting thinking that the initiating group does not want, need, or welcome his/her participation in the new group. The "welcome mat" thrown out by the initiating group includes:

- a clear and simple agenda given to each attendee at the start of the meeting;
- a sign-up sheet so that all attendees' contact information is collected;
- some simple refreshments;
- structure and facilitation that invite feedback and participation by all.

None of us can change the world on our own. It takes a movement to change the world; it takes organizations to build the movement; it takes working with others to birth and power organizations.

Political Action Needs Leadership

LGBT political action groups share a common mission: to change the social and political status of LGBT people so that none of us fear punishment, persecution, or prosecution for being who we are. Political action groups need three basic components to do the work:

1. a plan of action that strategically and effectively deploys the energy and resources of members, supporters, and constituents;
2. members who make the action possible and meaningful;
3. leaders who can lead the group.

Leaders in the LGBT movement vary widely in their skill sets, their capacities to lead others, and their abilities to think strategically. It is not uncommon for LGBT organizational leaders to rise from the ranks with no actual experience or formal training in how to lead an organization. In a relatively small social-change movement like ours, failures of leadership prompt charges of egotism, self-aggrandizement, self-interest, and bunker-mentality authoritarianism, rather than an acknowledgment that too many of our leaders learn on the job. Stepping up to the most visible position within movement organizations or projects, no matter how large or small the group or project, makes the leader a target. Our group leaders are not larger-than-life superheroes. They are women and men who need support and encouragement from a trusted circle of friends and advisers. In return, our group leaders need to listen as often as they talk and to consult many colleagues before they decide. The conundrum is this: Not all of us want to unite, motivate, inspire, and direct the energy and resources of a group of people toward accomplishing the goals we all want to reach, and yet leadership breathes life into our movement and our organizations.

Absent a coherent strategy for raising leaders who are supported to succeed, some of the best opportunities for leadership development can be found in internship/fellowship programs at our larger political organizations. Many of these programs offer a modest stipend or college course credit for short-term internships. For people, young or old, who can forgo a weekly paycheck, the internships give participants hands-on work experience in a social-movement organization, the chance to make meaningful contacts with staff members, résumé-building work, a bird's-eye view of life in a political movement, and the potential for recommendations to future employers both in and outside politics.

Organizational Angst Comes with the Territory

The LGBT social justice movement is energized largely by the work of volunteers, people who give willingly of their time and energy. Volunteer leaders, volunteer members, volunteer boards of directors, volunteer committee chairs and members, volunteer event organizers. When volunteers' nerves get frayed, they can take their energy elsewhere. In the LGBT movement, as in most human endeavors, we invariably frustrate one another, annoy one another, and delight in one another. Human beings are flawed instruments for communication; our minds and hearts are fraught with unspoken and unconscious motivations; we often react with fear and anxiety and protectiveness, rather than confidence and power and generosity. Any LGBT organization, in fact any community-based organization, will be riddled with human drama and interpersonal angst. It's the unavoidable dilemma of individual consciousness: no one can ever completely know or empathize with anyone else, and so we imperfectly interpret the behaviors of others. As activist leaders, it is our job to motivate, inspire, and help others imagine the creation of a better world and to work toward that despite the human foibles that will inevitably occur along the way. We need to deal honestly and openly and compassionately with our colleagues and peers, and also be bold about protecting and guiding the world-changing work in which we are engaged. We need to keep this work uppermost in our minds so that we and others around us remember that what is most important is the eradication of homophobia.

GAME PLAN FOR CHAPTER ONE
Coming Out

Coming out means acknowledging one's sexual orientation/gender identity and acting positively on that self-awareness. People come out at varying times of life and under widely different life circumstances. Many LGBT people note that coming out is a lifelong experience, since we constantly meet people who don't know and can't discern our sexual orientation or gender identity.

Coming Out: Twelve Steps to Personal Liberation

1. I acknowledge within myself that my sexual orientation brings me to states of attraction, love, affection, and desire for persons of my sex; (or) I acknowledge within myself that my gender identity differs from the construction of my physical body.
2. I come to appreciate that my sexual orientation/gender identity is fully and naturally and undeniably a part of who I am.
3. I decide to be true to who I am.
4. I examine the ways in which truth to myself can risk my current relationships.
5. I examine the ways in which truth to myself can invite new relationships into my life.
6. I step forward into a changed life by telling others that I am: a lesbian; a gay man; a bisexual person; a transgender person.
7. I ask those around me for support and understanding as I explore a changed life.
8. I am willing to hear from friends, family, and my loved ones what my declaration of sexual orientation/gender identity means to them.
9. I seek others like me.
10. I seek relationships with others like me.
11. I make myself fully aware of what my sexual orientation/gender identity means in the community and country in which I live.
12. I join with others to transform the community and country in which I live so that no others will be afraid to live true to their own sexual orientation/gender identity.

Resources for Coming Out

The resources listed here can help you in your own coming-out process, no matter what your current situation.

Parents, Families and Friends of Lesbians and Gays (PFLAG) is a national nonprofit organization with more than two hundred thousand members and supporters and more than five hundred affiliates in the United States. On the PFLAG Web site, you will find information and resources about the process of coming out. This site includes advice, tips, and information about parents and families of LGBT people. Who better than a group of parents and friends of openly and proudly LGBT people to guide us in the coming-out process, and to help our families through their own processes? After all, PFLAG is powered by the loving parents of people like us. Learn from the experts. Type "PFLAG" into your browser to visit their site.

The Human Rights Campaign Foundation, the educational arm of the Human Rights Campaign, a gay, lesbian, bisexual, and transgender civil rights organization, offers many resources about coming out, from a program called the National Coming Out Project to an annual day of coming-out activities called National Coming Out Day. The coming-out segment of the HRC Web site is a treasure trove of online and downloadable resources and information to support you and others. Of special note, the HRC Web site offers a Spanish-language version of the foundation's *Resource Guide to Coming Out*, as well as specialized guides for African Americans, Latinos/Latinas, and Asian Pacific Americans, as well as straight allies. National Coming Out Day is celebrated on October 11 each year. As well as providing a platform for a wide variety of coming-out events and celebrations, National Coming Out Day marks the anniversary of the 1987 March on Washington for Lesbian and Gay Rights. Type "Human Rights Campaign" into your browser and click on "Get Informed" and then "Coming Out."

Bisexual Resource Center, located in Boston, is one of only a few resource outlets by, for, and about bisexual people. A visit to the Web site will yield excellent printed resources about bisexuality: click on "Publications" to view the online pamphlets. You'll be richly rewarded. Set your browser for "bisexual resources."

Advocates for Youth is a Washington, D.C.–based organization that helps young people make informed and responsible decisions about their reproductive and sexual health. Advocates for Youth serves young people by boldly advocating for a more positive and realistic approach to adolescent sexual health. Advocates for Youth envisions a society that views sexuality as normal and healthy and treats young people as a valuable resource. Sounds good, doesn't it? You can find many useful brochures by and for youth at the organization's Web site, including a series of pamphlets titled *I Think I Might Be Gay [Lesbian, Bisexual, Transgender], Now What Do I Do?* Type "Advocates for Youth" into your search engine, then go to "Topics & Issues" and click on "Gay, Lesbian, Bisexual, Transgender, and Questioning (GLBTQ) Youth."

Resources For and About LGBT Youth

Since 1990, LGBT youth organizing has exploded onto the scene in most large metropolitan areas and in smaller communities around the United States. After we come out and while we are coming out, we need places to go and people to go with, right? Your favorite search engine will lead you to the support groups, service organizations, and resource outlets in your own community. The vast array of youth-oriented LGBT groups typically offer social activities and special events to build relationships and community, HIV/AIDS-prevention education, alcohol, drug, and tobacco risk-reduction programs, opportunities for cultural/artistic expression, health care referral, and sometimes meet more basic needs of young people like food, clothing, and housing. Increasingly, youth-oriented groups also offer political education about LGBT activism and leadership-skills training. Check out your nearest community or campus group. The resources listed here can help you find your way to a group near you.

   The National Youth Advocacy Coalition (NYAC) is a social justice organization that advocates for and with young people who are GLBTQ in an effort to end discrimination against these youth and to ensure their physical and emotional well-being. Many advocacy resources are available at the NYAC Web site and the annual NYAC youth summit is a must-attend for hundreds of youth leaders from around the United States. Type "NYAC" into your search engine to visit this site.

Advocates for Youth maintains a Web site by, for, and about LGBT youth with a search function for youth-related organizations and youth-serving organizations listed by state. The YouthResources Web site, a project of Advocates for Youth, has a strong emphasis on health and sexual-health issues. Be aware that the organizational database is a bit spotty, but nonetheless could be a good source for you. "Voices," a new section of the YouthResources site, celebrates art, poetry, stories, and essays by and for LGBT young people. Type "Advocates for Youth" into your browser to get to the site.

YOUTH.ORG is run by volunteers and was created to help self-identifying gay, lesbian, bisexual, and questioning youth. YOUTH .ORG provides young people with a safe space online to be themselves. Check it out. Express yourself. Connect with other young LGBT, queer, and questioning folk. Type "youth.org" in your search engine and you're on your way.

The Trevor Helpline is the only national twenty-four-hour, toll-free suicide-prevention hotline aimed at LGBT and sexual-identity-questioning youth. The Trevor Helpline helps those in crisis, or those wanting information on how to help a friend or loved one in crisis. Managed by San Francisco Suicide Prevention, Trevor Helpline calls are handled by highly trained counselors and are free and confidential. Call the helpline at (866) 4-U-TREVOR (488-7386), or type "Trevor Project" into your search engine.

Build Your Leadership Muscles

What is leadership? Does it refer only to persons in prominent positions? Is leadership a set of personal qualities? Does it mean having a special ability to mobilize others to action? Is leadership being willing to be the first person to enter a fray or struggle? Does leadership mean having the best and smartest ideas in the room? Or the most far-reaching vision of a solution and deepest analysis of a problem?

Leadership can be all of these things. But leadership also involves being willing to take action when you see that something needs doing. The most fundamental expression of leadership is *taking action*.

The LGBT political universe brims with leadership-building opportunities for interested and motivated people like you. LGBT political activity spans the full range of styles and venues in which to learn and practice organizing and advocacy. You can become involved in legislative lobbying and organizing, election campaigns for candidates or ballot questions on LGBT-related issues, visibility projects like Coming Out Day or marching with a group of LGBT people in your school's Homecoming parade, campus-based organizing, health and wellness projects, hobby or avocational groups, cultural and arts projects, communities of faith, organizing demonstrations to bring attention to an issue of pressing concern, public educational projects, pride event organizing, and providing social and support services to LGBT people in need. The possibilities are endless.

Nearly every existing LGBT group with staff and budget, irrespective of its mission, needs help. Most organizations offer a structured way to be involved, through internship or fellowship programs. These programs typically provide an opportunity to learn some aspect of the day-to-day operations of an organization, whether the focus of the internship is political organizing, administration, fund-raising, membership recruitment, or event organizing. Intern and fellowship programs build your skills, bring you into contact with LGBT professionals in the community and movement, add to your résumé, and sometimes actually pay a stipend or small salary. Interns and fellows sign on for a specific period of time with the host organization and are assigned to work with a staff person or become part of a team of interns working on a well-defined project. You can learn more about internship and fellowship programs by visiting the Web sites of LGBT organizations or by calling them to inquire.

Other ways to flex your leadership muscles include:

- volunteering with an organization, either on a regular schedule (once or twice a week) or by joining in at an organization's regular "volunteer night" when your schedule allows;
- offering to chair a committee on campus or with your favorite community group;

- working with a few friends to meet a need that you have identified in your community;
- pitching in on a political campaign;
- hosting a house party for your favorite group or candidate so that your friends can learn more and become more actively involved in what you care about;
- making a financial contribution to an organization or candidate that represents what you believe and works for the world you want;
- speaking up when you observe that another person is being treated unfairly.

An entire world of LGBT community and political organizing awaits you. Pick up the phone or click that mouse and get started. You will learn, you will grow, you will contribute to the social movement for LGBT people, and you may find out that working in the LGBT movement is what you really want to do.

Try This at Home: Organize a Gay-Straight Alliance at Your School

Gay-straight alliances (GSAs) have become a staple of campus-based organizing by, for, and about LGBT students. First launched in Massachusetts in the early 1990s, the GSA model has taken root in nearly every state in the country. There are more than a thousand campus-based LGBT student clubs in the United States. Many have been established within school environments where students, teachers, and administrators have been supportive and helpful. But some GSA organizers encounter resistance from school leaders and, occasionally, from parents of other students and community members. However, if a school is a public high school that receives federal financial assistance and allows noncurriculum-related student clubs to meet at school during nonclass time (any kind of club, even just one club), organizers of a GSA must be given equal access to the facilities and resources of the school. In other words, no matter how much the administration might oppose the organizing of a GSA or other LGBT student club, administrators are bound by law to give you the same kind of help they give to the students organizing any other kind of noncurriculum-related club. What the mountain-climbing club gets, what the future teachers club gets, what the Bible-study club gets, the GSA gets too.

Working within a college or university context is a bit different, primarily because college-age students are regarded as young adults, not children. The right of LGBT students to organize on campuses of publicly funded universities is, for the most part, well established. Student activities funds and resources become available through the assessment of students via the student activities fees structure. On college and university campuses, with the exception of private schools that restrict student expressions of minority sexual orientation or gender expression, establishing a GSA or other LGBT student club is typically much more straightforward than working within a high school. Begin finding out about the process of establishing a student organization on campus by contacting the student activities office or the student government office. It's also important to spend some time thinking about and discussing with a friend or two the climate that exists for such a group. There are no right answers to these questions, but thinking through the current situation of LGBT students at your school is well worth doing before you launch an organizing campaign to start a GSA. You may be surprised at what you and your friends learn about your school by talking with one another. Here are some things to think about when considering the launch of a school-based student organization.

- *Assess the existing support groups and social clubs at your school.* Become familiar with the groups and clubs that other students have started. Talk to some of the student leaders about how they started their groups and what kinds of support are available to groups at your school.
- *Ask other student leaders if openly LGBT students are welcome to participate in their groups, and what the level of LGBT participation is.* If student groups aren't welcoming to LGBT students, then starting a group for LGBT students becomes even more important. If

the student group leaders say that their organizations are welcoming but that no openly LGBT students participate, then this, too, is a good reason to go forward with a group for LGBT students.

- *Think about whether you and your friends have ever discussed the need or desire for a group for LGBT students.* If the subject has come up before in conversation, then you've got good reason to think that there will be strong interest in your group.
- *Consider if there are other students you know who might already be interested in such a group.* Whether these friends and acquaintances are LGBT or not, they may be ready, willing, and waiting for someone like you to start the ball rolling. Talk to people who you think might be interested, and ask them to support your organizing efforts by joining the GSA.
- *Keep track of incidents of anti-LGBT harassment, bullying, or even violence at your school.* If you know of students who have been victims of these kinds of incidents, ask them to write a brief description, including date, time, specific information about what happened, location, and any other details that will help you build the case that your school must be a safer place for all students.
- *Listen for the way that LGBT issues and topics are discussed in class, in the hallways, and at school events.* If you hear LGBT people being denigrated and insulted, or if there is silence in classes where LGBT issues could be discussed, such as in a social studies course, this, too, is evidence of the need for LGBT visibility and advocacy that can come from a GSA.
- *Pay attention to derogatory language.* If anti-LGBT epithets are used at your school, whether directed at specific individuals or used more generally, as in the phrase "That's so gay," make note of the contexts and frequency of their occurrence. You'll be able to use this information later as you make your case for a GSA.
- *Talk with openly LGBT teachers and staff about your idea to start a group for LGBT students.* Don't forget to include out straight allies. The supportive adults in your school environment will be important advocates for your project.

- *Think about the options for the kind of organization that meets your needs and what you'd like to have available at your school.* Some groups offer social opportunities, a place to give and get support in your coming-out process, and a gathering place for like-minded students ready to challenge homophobia in the hallways and classrooms. But you need not be limited by this short list; think about what you really want and need at your school and build an organization around that.
- *Find out if there are any other LGBT student clubs or GSAs in your community or state.* Student leaders at other schools in your region or state have perhaps already organized groups just like the one you're thinking about starting. These student leaders can offer support to you and serve as an invaluable source of advice and wisdom as you confront unfamiliar situations.

Resources for Organizing at the High School Level

There are three excellent Web resources for student organizing at the high school level: the Gay Straight Alliance Network; the Gay, Lesbian & Straight Education Network (GLSEN), and the Department of Education in Massachusetts. Each can be accessed by typing the organizational name into your Web browser.

Organizations Offering Internships, Fellowships, and Other Opportunities for Young Organizers

All these organizations can be reached at their Web sites; just type the organization name into your browser and go.

National Coalition of Anti-Violence Programs (NCAVP) is a coalition of over twenty lesbian, gay, bisexual, and transgender victim advocacy and documentation organizations.

BiNet USA, the National Bisexual Network, an umbrella organization and voice for bisexual people, facilitates the development of a network of bisexual communities, promotes bisexual visibility, and collects and distributes educational information regarding bisexuality.

L.A. Gay & Lesbian Center provides a broad array of services for the lesbian, gay, bisexual, and transgender community in the Los Angeles area.

National Association of LGBT Community Centers supports and enhances LGBT community centers. The Web site features a directory of community centers around the United States.

New York Lesbian, Gay, Bisexual, and Transgender Community Center provides a home for LGBT organizations, institutions, and culture; cares for individuals and groups in need; educates the public and the LGBT community; and empowers all to achieve their fullest potential.

Children of Lesbians & Gays Everywhere (COLAGE) engages, connects, and empowers people to make the world a better place for children of LGBT parents and families.

Family Pride Coalition is dedicated to equality for LGBT parents and their families.

Parents, Families and Friends of Lesbians and Gays (PFLAG) celebrates diversity and envisions a society that embraces everyone, including those of diverse sexual orientations and gender identities.

AIDS Action advocates for federal and state budget appropriations to fight the AIDS epidemic.

Gay and Lesbian Medical Association works to ensure equality in health care for LGBT individuals and health care professionals.

Mautner Project for Lesbians with Cancer supports lesbians with cancer and their loved ones. The Web site is in English and Spanish.

Pride at Work is a constituency group of the AFL-CIO that works to mobilize mutual support between organized labor and the LGBT community.

ACLU Lesbian & Gay Rights Project seeks equal treatment and equal dignity for LGBT people.

Lambda Legal Defense and Education Fund is the nation's oldest and largest legal organization working for the civil rights of lesbians, gay men, and people with HIV/AIDS.

National Center for Lesbian Rights is a national legal resource center with a primary commitment to advancing the rights and safety of lesbians and their families through litigation, public policy advocacy, and public education.

Servicemembers Legal Defense Network is a national organization devoted to assisting members of the U.S. Armed Forces who are affected by "Don't Ask, Don't Tell."

Equality Federation is a network of U.S. state and territory organizations committed to working together and with national and local groups to strengthen statewide advocacy for LGBT people.

Freedom to Marry is an American coalition committed to winning and keeping the freedom to marry for same-gender couples.

Gay & Lesbian Victory Fund provides financial and campaign support to gay and lesbian political candidates.

Gender Education & Advocacy, Inc. provides resources and activism for the transgender community.

Human Rights Campaign is a national GLBT political organization with members throughout the country.

National Center for Transgender Equality (NCTE) is a social justice organization dedicated to advancing the equality of transgender people.

National Gay and Lesbian Task Force is the oldest LGBT civil rights organization in the country and organizes broad-based campaigns to build public support for complete equality for LGBT people. Its Policy Institute, the community's premier think tank, provides research and policy analysis to support the struggle for complete equality.

National Log Cabin Republican Clubs is a national gay and lesbian Republican grassroots organization.

National Stonewall Democrats is a network of gay and lesbian Democratic clubs.

National Transgender Advocacy Coalition (NTAC) is a transgender civil rights organization.

The Institute for Gay and Lesbian Strategic Studies conducts research and analysis on issues important to LGBT Americans.

The **Williams Institute on Sexual Orientation Law and Public Policy** at the UCLA School of Law is a think tank supporting legal scholarship, legal research, policy analysis, and education regarding sexual-orientation discrimination and other legal issues that affect lesbian and gay people.

International Gay & Lesbian Human Rights Commission (IGLHRC) is an organization filling the gap between the international human rights movement and the gay rights movement.

Immigration Equality aims to help gay, bisexual, and lesbian immigrants and campaign for them.

Gay & Lesbian Alliance against Defamation (GLAAD) is dedicated to fair, accurate, and inclusive media representation as a means of eliminating homophobia and discrimination based on gender identity and sexual orientation.

Asian Equality (formerly APACE) is a national ad hoc coalition of Asian Pacific Islander leaders and organizations determined to fight marriage discrimination against our communities.

The Audre Lorde Project is a lesbian, gay, bisexual, two spirit (Native American phrase for LGBT people), and transgender people of color center for community organizing, focusing on the New York City area.

National Black Justice Coalition is a national civil rights organization of black LGBT people.

The National Latino/a Coalition for Justice fights to end discrimination in marriage.

National Minority AIDS Council (NMAC) is dedicated to developing leadership within communities of color to address HIV/AIDS.

Two Spirit Press Room is a GLBT Native American media and cultural literacy project.

Campus Pride is an online resource for LGBT organizers on college and university campuses.

National Consortium of Directors of LGBT Resources in Higher Education works to critically transform higher education environments so that LGBT students, faculty, administrators, staff, and alumni/ae have equity in every respect.

Gay, Lesbian & Straight Education Network (GLSEN) is an organization for students, parents, and teachers to effect positive change in schools. Offers information on what you can do in your state.

National Youth Advocacy Coalition improves the lives of LGBTQ youth through advocacy, education, and information.

2

What We Want
and What We Need

The particular form of abomination that shocked the sensibilities of our forefathers.

The abominable vice of buggery.

The detestable and abominable vice of buggery committed with mankind or beast.

The high displeasure of Almighty God.

The unnameable crime against nature.

That most horrid and detestable crime (among Christians not to be named) called sodomy.

The abominable crime not fit to be named among Christians.

Unseemly practices.

Unchaste behavior.

Perverted practices.

Sexual perversity.

Gross indecency.

Sexual psychopath.

Unnatural and perverted practices.

Abnormal sexual desires.

Unnatural sexual intercourse.

These are just some of the legal terms used to describe same-sex sexual behavior, terms that represent society's cruel and remorseless campaign to persecute, prosecute, and punish homosexuals, including men and women, young adults and elderly adults, in private and in semipublic, in long-term committed relationships or in simple consensual sexual assignations between temporary friends. Death by hanging, death by drowning, death at the burning pit, flogging, confinement in stocks and pillories, imprisonment, commitment to prisons for the mentally insane, beatings and murders, expulsion from military service, castrations, shock therapy, deprogramming and other forms of psychological abuse, humiliation through news accounts of arrests (sometimes followed by the suicide of the arrested person), removal of children from parents—all these have been considered to be just punishments or logical outcomes for transgressions of written and unwritten proscriptions against same-sex sexual relations. Lesbians, gay men, and bisexual people were and are hounded, hated, hunted, and harassed because we "do it that way."

In the United States, beginning with colonial law and continuing uninterrupted until 2003, the gears of the state criminal apparatus ground relentlessly in pursuit of "sexual criminals" who were consenting adults engaged in private acts of affection, desire, love, and sexuality, "crimes" without "victims." Beginning in 1961 with Illinois, lawmakers and courts in thirty-five states decriminalized or reformed laws punishing private, adult, consensual sex. On June 26, 2003, the U.S. Supreme Court, in *Lawrence v. Texas,* struck down the remaining fifteen state laws that named us criminals. Abruptly and with celebrations in LGBT communities around the country, the government's shameful reign of terror against the civilian practice of homosexuality came to an end. But harsh law and policy against expressions of same-sex desire and love remains the order of the day in the Uniform Code of Military Justice, which regulates the lives of American men and women in military service.

It is no wonder, then, that the earliest stirrings of political consciousness and action among our movement's founders fixed on ridding us of these terrible and ancient laws and prohibitions. Early LGBT organizations like the Mattachine Society, founded in 1951, and the Daughters of Bilitis, founded in 1955, understood that sexual repression by governmental authorities had to be resisted and stopped if LGBT people were ever to be free to live openly and proudly. While this yearning to be free was sometimes expressed as simply and merely wanting to be left alone, the attention of early activists always returned to the urgent work of repealing the myriad of criminal laws available to police, prosecutors, juries, and judges for the purpose of cleansing their communities of openly homosexual people. From prohibitions on sexual behavior to bans on soliciting another person for sex to criminalizing same-sex dancing, the cops and the criminal-justice system that stood behind them wielded immense power to silence, censor, and penalize expressions of homosexuality.

Against this deep state power to repress our people emerged the earliest political organizing on behalf of LGBT people, some of it done under the banner of the 1950s-style homophile organizations that were dedicated to setting up support networks for gay and lesbian people. But the idea of sexual liberation for homosexuals caught fire among some activist organizers who saw liberation as critically important to securing freedom for LGBT people, just as the concept of civil rights for descendants of black slaves had given rise to a call for the liberation of black Americans from the complicated social and cultural legacies of slavery. Gay liberation's central tenet was that the fundamental order of society must be transformed in order to free homosexuals and women from rigidly enforced sex roles and gender assignments so that both LGBT people and women would achieve full self-determination and control and integrity over their bodies. Gay liberation rhetoric brims with images of throwing off the chains of oppression to be free from the bonds of sex-typed gender roles. The Gay Liberation Front in New York City proclaimed, in its statement of purpose in late 1969: "We are a revolutionary group of men and women formed with the realization that complete sexual liberation for all people cannot come about unless existing social institutions are abolished. We reject society's attempt to impose sexual roles and definitions of our nature."

Much like their sisters in the women's liberation movement and the activists of the black liberation movement, organizers in the gay liberation movement employed consciousness-raising and direct-action tactics to both engage in self-education about the demeaned social status of homosexuals and to challenge that status by confronting institutions such as the media, the church, and the state. The glory days of gay liberation theory and practice tracked closely with the movements for the liberation of black people and women. As the revolutionary fervor and enthusiasm for the hippie counterculture of the 1960s waned, a more reformist style of organizing, framed around gay rights and civil rights, eclipsed gay liberation by the early 1970s, setting off a decades-long debate over the validity and legitimacy of gay liberation versus gay rights strategies.

The apparent contradiction between gay liberation on the one hand and gay rights on the other crystallizes around issues of sexuality. Proponents of gay rights are seen by gay liberationists as stodgy, conservative, fear-driven people who seek to repress their sexualities in order to imitate and kowtow to the dominant heterosexual society's values exemplified by middle-class suburban churchgoing life. The gay liberationists are characterized by gay legal reformers as dinosaurs and throwbacks to the heady days of the sexual revolution, embarrassing to the equality-driven movement and adolescent remnants of failed revolutionary ideology. Both of these views are wrong. Reformist projects to win full legal and social equality and a more rambunctious segment of the movement devoted to sexual freedom, agency, and integrity are equally vital to the survival of LGBT people. Humans need and want to enjoy sex and sexuality, free from meddling government agencies and from fear of more-informal kinds of persecution such as gay-bashing. At the same time, having achieved the freedom to be, act, and love queer, we inevitably collide with the need to organize our lives and our living in much the same way as our straight neighbors, siblings, and coworkers. We need to work to earn a living; we need a safe home and neighborhood in which to live; we need to become educated to function in society; we need to take care of children and adults who rely on us. Food, clothing, shelter, education, and caring for others are not needs that are unique to any group of people. The straights need all of this; the lesbians need all of this; the gay men need all of this; the transgender people need all of this; the bisexual people need all of this.

The legacy of sodomy laws, which have been described as the linchpin of anti-LGBT discrimination, prevents us from securing the basic needs of life for ourselves and our loved ones. Centuries of criminalizing our sexual behavior opened the door to uncountable acts of state-sponsored and privately administered discrimination. LGBT people are still denied jobs, housing, education, and access to public spaces and public resources, and endure attacks on their relationships and their families. Until *Lawrence,* much of the justification for this discrimination rested on denying criminals, unconvicted or otherwise, the rights and benefits of society. After *Lawrence,* we can pursue the as-yet-incomplete struggle to ban arbitrary discrimination, free of the burden of criminality of the very act that can define us as gay, lesbian, or bisexual. No city council member, no legislator, no judge, no editorial writer can use the cudgel of sodomy laws against us as we seek access to the basic means to secure life, liberty, and the pursuit of happiness. *Lawrence* not only freed us from sodomy laws; it ushered in a new era in which we are entitled to and can demand the respect of political and social institutions.

Still, our glass of equality sits less than half full. About half of lesbian, gay, and bisexual people in the United States live in states without any legal protections for their rights to earn a living, rent a home, get an education, or have equal access to public accommodations. Transgender people face a much grimmer picture: only eight states ban discrimination on the basis of gender expression as well as sexual orientation. Nine states outlaw discrimination on the basis of sexual orientation only, making a total of seventeen states with some form of protection. In thirty-three states, however, LGBT people live, work, and go to school with no legal recourse in instances of denial of basic rights. Large swaths of the United States are empty of protections for any of us. Only one state, Massachusetts, grants to same-sex couples the right to marry, thus giving us access to the most simple and straightforward route to recognition of our next-of-kin status and the capacity to care for our immediate family members.

Despite being introduced annually since 1975, federal legislation to protect us against discrimination has been approved by the U.S. Senate only once, in 1996. That vote to pass a federal rights bill for LGBT people left a bitter taste: it had been amended to a federal bill to ban recognition of marriages between persons of the same sex, which also passed the Senate. The federal Defense of Marriage Act later won approval by the House of Representatives and President Bill Clinton signed it into law under darkest night and without any ceremony. The nondiscrimination legislation never received consideration by the House, much less the president's signature. Likewise, the federal government has yet to enact legislation to include violent, bias-driven crimes against LGBT people for federal investigation and prosecution.

Changes in law will not bring us freedom, but changes in law will bring us fairness and equality. Each of us wins our freedom when we come out and refuse to live silently and secretly and when we determine for ourselves whom and how we will love. But sweeping societal changes in attitudes and perceptions of LGBT people are reflected in changes in law. Our laws define and govern how we treat one another and how our government treats and cares for each of us. Laws express the value that society places on our lives. Laws require that people be treated as equals. The end of the regime of sodomy laws articulated that, finally, our right to have sex with another person of the same sex would be respected by government entities. We now must extend that respect for our sexuality to winning full legal and social equality for ourselves and our families.

The mechanisms for securing full equality are found in representative and participatory democracy: the town councils, the county commissions, the state legislatures; the free press; the public square; the social movements standing alongside workers, women, people of color, disabled people, religious groups, children, immigrants, and, yes, lesbians, gay men, transgender people, and bisexual people. The LGBT social movement engages the political decision-making process at every level and has achieved considerable success since the first gay and lesbian nondiscrimination legislation was enacted in Alfred, New York, in 1974.

The late, great U.S. congressman and House Speaker Thomas P. "Tip" O'Neill said it best: "All politics is local." For the LGBT political movement, the essential work of building a solid foundation at the local level cannot be ignored. Beginning in the early 1970s, LGBT activist leaders sought to enact local nondiscrimination laws that protect people from arbitrary acts of discrimination on the basis of sexual orientation and gender identity. While the first laws did not include gender expression, as the movement evolved to include transgender people, a wave of local and state laws banning discrimination on the basis of gender expression began in local communities in the mid-1990s. By concentrating first on local campaigns, organizers accomplished several crucial goals: educating voters and opinion leaders about the reality of discrimination; learning from firsthand experience how to work within the political system; building solid working relationships with local political leaders; demonstrating to elected officials in higher offices that standing with LGBT people was the right thing to do and would not create a backlash against them; and generating LGBT power at the local, grassroots level.

The importance of working with local elected officials cannot be overemphasized. Democracy's arithmetic is quite simple: of nearly 500,000 elected officials in the United States, only 542 hold federal offices. We elect 1 president, 1 vice president, 100 U.S. senators (2 from each state), 435 U.S. representatives, 4 delegates to the House of Representatives from U.S. territories and the District of Columbia, and 1 resident commissioner from the Commonwealth of Puerto Rico. We elect the remaining 499,458 elected officials to posts at the state, county, and local levels of government, with the vast majority at the local level.

Local elected officials spend the bulk of their governance time on public education, infrastructure issues like garbage collection and street repair, zoning and development concerns, and maintaining parks, but they also have the power to enact local laws protecting rights of residents that go far beyond the civil rights laws of the federal government. (State legislatures, too, can enact civil rights protections that exceed what the federal laws mandate.) We make faster progress and go much further by starting in our own town and city councils and with our mayors than by starting with the U.S. Congress and the president, because the sweeping legal and political change we seek, which is still regarded as experimental, controversial, and even radical, requires support on a sturdy foundation. Some local elected officials with whom we work on nondiscrimination ordinances inevitably seek higher office, some to the state legislature or to statewide office and some to the U.S. Congress. The members of Congress who did *not* start their political careers in the city council or on the local school board or in the state legislature are the exceptions, not the rule. Tip O'Neill served on the Cambridge (Massachusetts) School Committee, after losing his first campaign for a seat on the Cambridge City Council. O'Neill, and every elected official who ascends the political ladder, understood that the relationships made while serving in more humble offices are carried into all higher offices. When we work with local elected officials on LGBT issues, we are creating relationships that will pay off for us in the future, because no elected official wants to lose support from civic leaders and voters in his/her home community. We can reasonably expect lawmakers who vote with us on a local nondiscrimination law to vote with us again, because they have staked out a position of support for LGBT people.

LGBT activists waged the fight to repeal the antisodomy laws at the state level because it is the state legislatures that set laws relating to most criminal activities, including crimes involving sex. Similarly, with only rare and important exceptions, state courts determine the constitutional validity of laws enacted by state legislatures. Campaigns and projects to repeal or reform sodomy laws, whether legislative or judicial, are conducted within state governmental contexts. Prior to the 2003 U.S. Supreme Court decision in *Lawrence v. Texas* that struck down all existing sodomy laws, state legislatures and state courts comprised the battlegrounds for sodomy-law struggles. Fifty states, fifty battles, and an urgent need for fifty strong statewide political organizations to carry the workload.

While our movement founders recognized the importance of challenging state control over the lives of LGBT people by expunging sodomy laws and other related statutes from the books, the LGBT political movement of the 1950s was, in its infancy, not much more than an idea.

Early LGBT organizers focused much of their energy on the formation of nascent support groups, first for gay men and then later for lesbians. The Mattachine Society and Daughters of Bilitis, both founded in large California cities, spawned chapter groups in other large urban areas, but neither group constituted a centralizing and consolidating force for political change. Even without forceful political organizing by the existing gay and lesbian groups, a legal-reform organization called the American Law Institute (ALI) in 1955 published its Model Penal Code, which sought to standardize aspects of state criminal law. The ALI Model Penal Code dropped sodomy from its list of crimes, rationalizing that crimes without victims were not really crimes and that the lack of medical clarity about homosexuality as a disease or genetic condition supported the removal of sodomy as criminal behavior. The ALI also recognized that sodomy, most commonly practiced in private, occurred well beyond the reach of the law. With few discernible efforts by LGBT activists, beginning in Illinois in 1961, state legislatures tossed sodomy laws into the dustbins as the Model Penal Code was adopted. By 1977, eighteen states had legislatively repealed sodomy laws and another seven states decriminalized heterosexual consensual sodomy, but specifically criminalized homosexual consensual sodomy. Nevertheless, even in states that repealed sodomy laws, police still had the power and authority to harass and arrest men and women for violations of the solicitation laws that banned asking another person to engage in sexual activity.

While the adoption of the Model Penal Code quietly repealed sodomy laws in a dozen and a half states and led to homosexual-specific bans on sex between consenting adults in private, the relatively weak and locally organized LGBT organizations and LGBT communities around the country took root and grew. The more celebrated Stonewall Rebellion in New York in 1969 had been preceded in 1966 by an infamous incident at Compton's Cafeteria in San Francisco during which transgender people and transvestites fought back against the cops who had conducted a months-long campaign of harassment and arrests against them for assembling in a public place. Gay activists in Los Angeles organized demonstrations in 1967 to protest police raids on bars there. Each of these epiphanic events, each taking place in different cities with strong LGBT communities but at roughly the same moment in movement history, inspired other LGBT people to join together in active resistance to the many expressions of hatred and scorn for lesbians, gay men, and bisexual and transgender people.

This great upsurge in LGBT organizing resulted in new political and legal formations, including the National Gay Task Force and Lambda Legal Defense and Education Fund, both founded in 1973. New groups like these went far beyond their antecedents of the 1950s and 1960s in that they were national in scope and launched projects to challenge institutional homophobia, including the repeal of sodomy laws. But the strategies deployed to challenge sodomy laws in the 1970s and mid-1980s were primarily litigable. Attorneys at Lambda and the American Civil Liberties Union and its state chapters successfully challenged sodomy laws in New York and Pennsylvania. With these victories in hand, attorneys hunkered down to pursue a larger strategy that would eventually bring a Georgia sodomy prosecution challenge all the way to the U.S. Supreme Court. Predicated on the theory that arguing for the privacy of adults engaging in consensual sodomy could be the key to overturning sodomy laws across the nation, Georgia's *Bowers v. Hardwick* was thought to be a strong contender before the nine justices of the Rehnquist Court, led by Chief Justice William Rehnquist. But the Court's June 30, 1986, decision upheld the right of states to criminalize sodomy between persons of the same sex. It landed like a neutron bomb in LGBT communities around the country. By the slimmest possible majority vote of 5–4, the Court declared that homosexuals had no constitutionally protected right to engage in private adult consensual sexual behavior. What the bar raids had been to the 1960s political movement for LGBT freedom and dignity, *Hardwick* was to our movement of the 1980s. LGBT people poured into the streets to howl their rage. In New York, four thousand people stopped traffic that Fourth of July weekend. In Boston, activists gathered for a protest at the Massachusetts State House, "kissing-in for liberty" and demanding that the Massachusetts legislature repeal that state's colonial-era sodomy statute. Hundreds of San Franciscans demonstrated against the decision when Supreme Court justice Sandra Day O'Connor spoke in that city in July. O'Connor, who had cast the fifth vote supporting the majority in *Hardwick*, drew LGBT wrath again in December 1986 when she made a public appearance at the University of Pennsylvania. Editorial pages in major newspapers across the country blasted the decision, deriding the Court for invading the privacy of adult citizens and for citing "millennia of moral teaching" as a rationale for upholding sodomy laws.

The confluence of the Court's decision in *Hardwick* and the rampaging AIDS epidemic brought the tempers of LGBT people and activists to a boiling point. While President Ronald Reagan ignored the emergent crisis of AIDS and refused to engage in effective life-saving AIDS-prevention education and condom distribution, the judicial branch of governments sanctioned the labeling of LGBT people as unconvicted sex criminals. The fury unleashed by the double whammy of AIDS denial from the White House and the insulting and injurious *Hardwick* decision from the Court demanded organizing, leadership, and action. Fifteen months after *Hardwick,* more than three hundred thousand LGBT people from all over the United States converged on Washington, D.C., for the second national March on Washington for Lesbian and Gay Rights, held on October 11, 1987. The event was bracketed by deep grief over the deaths of thousands of gay men to AIDS, as represented by the AIDS Memorial Quilt, displayed on vast acres of the great lawn on Washington's National Mall. The march enabled us to express our grief as a community, but also provided multiple opportunities for venting our outrage about the burgeoning AIDS crisis and the *Hardwick* decision. Two days after the march, on Monday, October 13, more than five thousand people demonstrated at the U.S. Supreme Court, and more than six hundred civil-disobedience demonstrators were taken into custody by the D.C. police for refusing to vacate the Court's front steps. The demonstration protesting the *Hardwick* decision marked the first time in the Court's history that it was forced by a mass protest on its steps to shut down operations for a day. Michael

Hardwick, whose name and story of arrest for sodomy in his Atlanta bedroom provided a dignified counterpoint to the disgraceful decision, participated in that day's civil-disobedience action. In an instance of delicious poetic justice, Hardwick was arrested at the U.S. Supreme Court while protesting the Court's decision justifying his arrest for having private adult consensual sex.

Following *Hardwick,* the National Gay and Lesbian Task Force voiced its fury by initiating a grassroots organizing project to repeal sodomy laws in the twenty-five states that retained them at the time of ruling. Although the *Hardwick* decision upheld existing sodomy laws, the Court's ruling did not mandate that states *must* criminalize sodomy, only that states *were permitted to* criminalize sodomy. The Task Force, then staffed by a half dozen women and men, raised funds by mailing directly to members and supporters a vivid pink map of the United States that divided the country into "free" and "unfree" states and promised to dispatch an organizer into the unfree states to inspire LGBT people to take action against the sodomy laws. I was hired late in 1986 to run the National Gay and Lesbian Task Force Privacy Project, an unprecedented campaign to build organizational strength and political capacity in some of the least organized states in the country, namely the southeastern and western states. The Privacy Project's two other goals were to produce useful organizing materials about sodomy-law repeal and to work in partnership with existing organizations in unfree states on their repeal efforts. One significant difference in how the Privacy Project approached sodomy-law repeal, in contrast to earlier, quieter strategies, was to ignite a discussion among lesbians and gay men about sex and sexuality. At the 1987 March on Washington, the Task Force hosted a first-ever "Town Meeting on Sex and Politics," at which eight hundred people crammed into an auditorium to listen to a panel of community thinkers discuss the juncture of sexuality, sex repression by the state, and sexual freedom for LGBT people. More than a dozen of these events around the country over the course of three years gave us a chance to talk among ourselves about the meaning, value, and significance of sex in our lives, the formal and informal ways that our sexuality was attacked, and the importance of repealing laws that codified homophobia.

Talking among ourselves, however, would not repeal sodomy laws. For that, we needed to talk to legislators. The Task Force identified a handful of states that posed "best chances" for successful repeal, including Michigan, Maryland, and Minnesota. Repeal strategies were plotted out for Minnesota and Maryland. Organizers in Michigan, which at the time boasted one of the more impressive statewide organizations, called the Michigan Organization for Human Rights, elected not to pursue a repeal campaign, focusing instead on nondiscrimination initiatives. In New Hampshire, an effort to recriminalize sodomy got under way early in 1987. The Privacy Project worked directly and closely with activists in the three legislatively vigorous states: Minnesota, Maryland, and New Hampshire. Legislative committees in each state held hearings, with the recriminalization bill in New Hampshire going down to swift defeat in committee. In Minnesota, the Senate Judiciary Committee was chaired by the openly gay senator Allan Spear. After a day of defamatory, sexually explicit testimony by the proponents of the sodomy law and objective, privacy-based arguments offered by the opponents of the sodomy law, the bill to repeal the Minnesota law was passed by the Senate committee. On the House side, however, the measure died in committee and was never voted on by the full body in either the Senate or the House. At the time, I wrote, in an article published in the journal *Radical America*: "Gay sex had been maligned and insulted, called criminal, immoral, unnatural, repulsive and sinful and we had not spoken out in defense of ourselves and our sexuality. Worse yet, this uncontested denigration of our sexuality had led to defeat of sodomy repeal in Minnesota." By limiting our testimony and our arguments for repeal to the language of privacy, separation of church and state, decriminalizing the sexuality of disabled persons, many of whom, by dint of physical limitations, engaged in oral sex, and reducing interference in AIDS-prevention education, we had avoided public discussion of our most heartfelt argument against sodomy laws: that the real crime of those laws was the denigration and criminalization of the sexualities of millions of people, and by extension, the criminalization of gay, lesbian, and bisexual people themselves. We had failed to bring a full-throated defense of our sexual communities to those who could decide to uncouple criminal law and our sexual behavior.

When the sodomy-repeal bill came before Maryland legislators, lawmakers indicated to the activists that the bill might win passage if it included a legislative preamble that expressly disavowed sexual conduct outside marriage and explicitly endorsed marriage as the foundation of society and family. This type of legislative preamble contributed to the successful repeal of the Wisconsin sodomy law in 1985. At the risk of losing the repeal of Maryland's sodomy laws, Maryland activists and outside advocates, myself among them, decided against that compromise offer from lawmakers. The bill went down to defeat.

Refusing to "go along to get along" with lawmakers around issues of sexuality and affirmations of LGBT human dignity remained a hallmark of the Privacy Project's work. At a 1990 rally held on the opening day of the Georgia legislature, activists arrived at the rally with a large brass bed, on which inflatable dolls simulated the sexual acts banned by Georgia law. At a civil-disobedience action later in the day, same-sex couples lay in the roadways, embracing and kissing. In a speech to the rally at the Georgia State House, I said, "We make a particular demand today that states not only repeal these odious statutes, but also apologize to us for the unpardonable offense of defining us as a sexually criminal class of citizens." Although some legislative advocates who wanted a quieter and less bombastic campaign to repeal the sodomy law later claimed that the demonstration had doomed the repeal bill, there were equally vociferous claims that repeal of Georgia's sodomy law was so unlikely to be achieved that a direct engagement with homophobic slander of homosexual behavior could be one way to stake out a more proud and spirited resistance to the ongoing defamations of our communities.

Not a single sodomy law was legislatively repealed during the working years of the Task Force Privacy Project, 1986–1991. But in addition to sparking a lively intracommunity discussion about gay and lesbian sexuality and working directly with organizers in a handful of states on legislative campaigns, the project helped to birth new political organizations in a half dozen states, some of these focused specifically on challenging the sodomy law in their states, others adopting a broader and more varied agenda for political action. Nevada and the District of Columbia both repealed their sodomy laws in 1993, Rhode Island did so in 1998, and Arizona in 2001. Kentucky in 1992, Tennessee in 1996, Montana in 1997, Georgia in 1998, and Minnesota in 2001 struck down their sodomy laws through state court actions.

The U.S. Supreme Court, in its 2003 majority opinion in *Lawrence,* ultimately spoke with the last word on the topic of sodomy laws in the United States. The Court's view best expressed the 180-degree turnaround in our collective understandings about sodomy laws and freedom. Justice Anthony Kennedy wrote the majority opinion and concluded, "*Bowers* was not correct when it was decided, and it is not correct today. It ought not to remain binding precedent. *Bowers v. Hardwick* should be and now is overruled." In stirring language, Kennedy wrote, "The petitioners are entitled to respect for their private lives," and "The state cannot demean their existence or control their destiny by making their private sexual conduct a crime."

In *Lawrence,* after nearly fifty years of organizing, advocating, lobbying, arguing before courts low and high, talking, writing, and singing out our anthems about sexual freedom and liberation, *Bowers v. Hardwick* fell and our lives were fully and finally vindicated from the seemingly endless campaign of terror against those whose love was too despicable to be named.

GAME PLAN FOR CHAPTER TWO
Sodomy Laws

The history of sodomy laws in the United States and around the world reveals much about how homosexuality and homosexual people have been understood and misunderstood. One excellent online resource about these laws and important court decisions in the United States, lovingly maintained by a group of activists living in Washington, D.C., the Sodomy Laws Web site tells us everything we ever wanted to know about sodomy laws and a lot more. Typing the phrase "sodomy laws" into your search engine will display this group's Web site, and many others with background information about sodomy laws in the United States and around the world.

What's Your State's Status on the Issues?

The Web site of the National Gay and Lesbian Task Force posts several excellent maps of the United States that show the differences from state to state regarding sodomy laws, nondiscrimination laws, and laws about domestic violence and bias crimes. To learn more about sodomy laws, pre– and post–*Lawrence v. Texas,* and nondiscrimination laws, you can also visit the Beacon Press Web site. Type these organizational names into your search engine to view the maps and find out how your state measures up to other states.

Try This at Home: Visit an Elected Official

Something is coming up that the student government will decide on or the city council will decide on and you have a strong opinion about it. There is no better time to meet with the elected officials who will make the decision, to share your views, ask what he/she thinks about the issue, and request support for your position. Elected officials, at any level of representative government from student council to the federal government, are accountable to the people who put them in office. They care about what voters think. Here are some things to think about when meeting with an elected official.

- *Do your homework.* Learn about the issue that is motivating you. Talk to other people about it. Listen to or read about views that are different from your own. Do research to fill in any information gaps about the issue.
- *Contact the elected official to request a time to meet.* Be as flexible with your own schedule as you can be, offering a few different

times to get together. Be clear that you want to discuss a specific issue that's on your mind. Be persistent about making an appointment, because this shows the official that you are serious about the issue and serious about wanting to meet.

• *Show up for the meeting on time.* Respect the official's schedule by agreeing at the outset how much time you and he or she will spend together.

• *Get to the point.* You've come to talk with the official about a specific issue, so don't waste time by talking about something else. State your case, explaining what your position is, why you hold that position, and why it's important that you receive support for your position. Be clear and concise. Make the issue personal by talking about how it affects you, your friends, your neighborhood, your community.

• *Ask for the official's opinion on the issue.* This individual has listened to your views, so return the courtesy. Make notes, mental or jotted down on paper, of what points you want to discuss further.

• *Respond to the official's views by specifically explaining your agreement or disagreement, without engaging in argument.* You may disagree on the issue of the day, but there may be opportunities in the future when you can agree and support each other. You're building a relationship with another person, so keeping your cool even when faced with a difference of opinion can leave the door open for future discussions.

• *Ask for the official's support or vote on the issue.* Even if what has been said by the individual rules out support for your view, ask for that support. Elected officials sometimes can find a way to offer partial support for your view, or are open to compromise or further consideration of an issue.

• *Thank the official for taking the time to meet with you.* Offer your assurance that you will be paying attention to how the individual votes or acts on the issue. If appropriate, send a written note briefly recapping your conversation and thanking the person for his or her time.

Try This at Home: Run for Office

Consider running for an elected office in your organization, in your school or on campus, or in your community. We live in a representative democracy with a popularly elected government that was designed to be run by the people, for the people, and of the people. Running for office is one way to take a more active role in an organization, school, community, state, or nation. By running for office, you will experience life as a candidate, planning and running a campaign. To be successful, you'll need to present your reasons for running, your goals, and what you want to accomplish if elected, and the compelling reasons why the eligible voters should support you over all other candidates. Here are some things to consider when contemplating running for office.

- *Choose a position to run for.* What job within your organization, on your campus, or in your community interests you? What are the qualifications for the position? What specific qualifications would you bring to the job? Have you been a visible leader already, or can you become a visible leader?
- *Ensure that you're up for the commitment.* Consider whether you have the time to devote to a campaign, and if elected, whether you have the time to do the job. Does the job fit into your life, your school schedule, your work schedule? Can you do what it takes to conduct a good campaign?
- *Identify your base.* Will your friends, family, and colleagues be behind you? Running for any office means asking people for support. If you ask for help, will enough people respond?
- *Think about why you're running.* What specific issues will you highlight in your campaign? Why will voters support you in preference to other candidates? In what ways have current officeholders failed to address the issues that you care about? Are the issues of most interest to you going to appeal to the people who can elect you?
- *Consider the larger context.* What will it take to win? How many

votes do you need to be successful? What other candidates are likely to run? Can you develop a slate of candidates and run on common themes, building a broader coalition of support?

• *Find out how to make it official.* What do you need to do to enter the race? How do you get your name on the ballot or list of nominated candidates? Research what kinds of papers need to be filed with what entities.

• *Assess your resources.* How much money is required to mount an effective campaign? What kinds of materials, stickers, posters will you need? How will these be produced and distributed? Are there candidates running for other positions with whom you can share resources?

• *Decide how you'll get the word out.* How will you have direct contact with the electorate? What is the best way to reach the people who actually cast votes in the election? Are there media outlets that will cover the campaign? How can you utilize media to support your candidacy?

Having considered running for office yourself, you may decide to go forward or you may give your support to others who are willing to be candidates. If you're not ready to make the commitment to run for office, think about volunteering on a campaign. Volunteering to help someone else run is a great way to learn more about campaigns and to develop friendships with other people who care about the issues that have motivated you to get involved. If your candidate gets elected, that individual will be very attuned to your opinions and views about issues going forward. After all, you just invested your time and energy to get him or her elected.

Resources for the LGBT Movement

You can find out much more about policies and laws that affect LGBT people. Using your search engine, type in any of the following phrases to visit educational sites, including the sites of groups that routinely oppose initiatives proposed by LGBT advocates. Try "sodomy laws," "gay rights laws," "LGBT nondiscrimination," and any variation of the following: "gay movement," "gay and lesbian movement," "LGBT movement," "bisexual movement," or "transgender movement." Many online sources provide both historical and contemporary information and views about all sectors of the LGBT movement.

3

How We Became
God-Fearin', Kid-Rearin',
Upstandin' Citizens

LGBT people are engaged in an epic struggle over who defines us, how we are defined, and how images can tell our truths and advance our political agendas. The struggle is revealed in how we understand and present ourselves in the media, to decision makers, and to ourselves, and the resulting backlash by our political adversaries, who seek to manipulate and distort our lives, our aspirations, and our relationships. In a culture as dependent on mass media as is contemporary U.S. society, enormous damages and enormous gains are at stake in the battle over how our communities are portrayed. Popular television and films serve as primary contemporary shapers of social realities and public consciousness about many political issues, including those affecting LGBT people and communities. But it was the news media, both electronic and print, that framed the way Americans viewed LGBT people from pre-Stonewall organizing through the early years of AIDS hysteria. Our political movement's progress has been deeply affected by a consistent narrative that "homosexual" means "sexual predator." This narrative supports and upholds the ideology of LGBT people as untrustworthy individuals driven by out-of-control sexual compulsions, and comprises the subtext of nearly all of our political struggles, both historical and contemporary.

In 1950s post–World War II America, social and cultural dynamics collided with and nearly swamped the infant LGBT liberation movement. Political anxieties ran high as the Cold War, a power struggle between the superpowers of the United States and the Soviet Union for ideological and economic world dominance, began to take shape in

America as virulent anti-Communism, at both elite and grassroots levels of society. At all levels of government, but especially the federal government, civil servants and public employees became targets of witch hunts against suspected Communist infiltrators and Communist sympathizers. Public-sector workers were expected to declare their allegiance to the U.S. government in so-called loyalty oaths, stating that they did not and would not advocate the overthrow of the government, nor were they members of any organization that advocated overthrow of the government. The failure to take a loyalty oath could result in the loss of a job.

Perverts, Communists, Traitors

While the loyalty oaths themselves pertained to antigovernment political activity, especially membership in the Communist Party, a series of events connected homosexuals with Communism and disloyalty to the government. Whittaker Chambers, an editor at *Time* magazine and a spy for the Soviet Union, was rumored to be gay and had told the Federal Bureau of Investigation (FBI) that he had ceased his homosexual activities once he left the Communist Party. When Chambers accused Alger Hiss, then president of the Carnegie Endowment for International Peace and a former official at the State Department, of spying for the Soviet Union, media coverage alluded to Chambers's secret attraction to Hiss. Hiss stood trial twice on charges of perjury that arose during his testimony before the House Un-American Activities Committee (HUAC). Hiss had requested that he be allowed to testify to HUAC so that he could refute Chambers's charges that he acted as a Soviet spy. But when Hiss testified before HUAC, the young California congressman Richard Nixon detected what he believed to be Hiss's lies concerning Chambers's assertion that he and Hiss were part of a ring of Soviet spies. Hiss was first acquitted of perjury, but at a later trial he was convicted of two counts of lying to a House of Representatives committee, and he was shadowed by the unsubstantiated accusation of spying for the Soviet Union. The Hiss-Chambers trials and surrounding media hoopla linked homosexuality, perjury, and treasonous activities by members of the Communist Party who worked in and had access to government documents. Then, in 1951, two British gay men, both Soviet spy suspects, defected to the Soviet Union, further cementing in the public imagination a link between homosexuality and treasonous Communist sympathies, including spying for the Soviet Union.

Republican senator Kenneth Wherry of Nebraska was quoted in the *New York Post* in December 1950 as stating: "You can't hardly separate homosexuals from subversives. . . . Mind you, I don't say that every homosexual is a subversive, and I don't say every subversive is a homosexual. But [people] of low morality are a menace in the government, whatever [they are], and they are all tied up together."

Sexual Psychopaths

These spectacular and notorious media events, together with a more generalized postwar social anxiety over the roles of women and a nascent visibility of gay and lesbian people, ignited a "sex panic" that swept the country, with public charges that sexual "deviates" had infiltrated the government and would or had already revealed state secrets to our Communist enemies. At the U.S. Department of State, several dozen employees were fired because of homosexual activities, resulting in a U.S. Senate–authorized investigation, Employment of Homosexuals and Other Sex Perverts in Government, by the Committee on Expenditures in the Executive Departments. In 1950, a report resulting from the investigation claimed, "These perverts will frequently attempt to entice normal individuals to engage in perverted practices. . . . One homosexual can pollute a government office." Because the insinuation that a person was homosexual was widely regarded as defamation of his/her character, gay people were also seen as especially vulnerable to blackmail and subsequent recruitment by foreign spies. President Dwight Eisenhower in 1953 signed an executive order that barred homosexuals from all federal jobs. The FBI set up surveillance systems to keep LGBT people out of government service and the U.S. military stepped up its efforts to purge openly gay and lesbian people from the ranks of the armed forces.

At the local level, police vice squads heard the vicious antigay message and harassed women and men who gathered in known gay-friendly nightspots, resulting in mass arrests of patrons. The ongoing police rampages through gay bars would ignite the Stonewall Rebellion in New York City in 1969, as well as other important but lesser-known acts of resistance to police aggressions, but in the early 1950s many homosexuals strived to stay underground and remain, as much as possible, unnoticed by neighbors, coworkers, and even family members. But the sex panic raging in Washington, D.C., reverberated through the lives of gay men who lived far from the nation's capital, who did not work in the public sector, and who had never visited a public gathering spot for homosexuals. These men were swept up in public antigay campaigns in smaller cities in the interior of the country where anxieties coalesced around a few sensational sexual assaults and murders of children and the alleged sexual exploitation of youth by gay men. In Boise, Idaho, a fifteen-month investigation in 1955 followed the arrest of three gay men on charges of sexual activity with teenagers. The Boise campaign against gay men included rounding up fourteen hundred residents for interrogation, with thirteen more gay men arrested and charged with "lewd and lascivious conduct" or "infamous crimes against nature." Ten were jailed, some without trial. In Sioux City, Iowa, a 1955 roundup of "sexual deviants" netted twenty men who were declared to be criminal sexual psychopaths and incarcerated at a state mental hospital for an indefinite period of time. The sexual-psychopath law under which the Sioux City men were incarcerated had been passed by Iowa legislators in response to the unsolved abduction of a young boy. The law stipulated that anyone who had "criminal propensities toward the commission of sex offenses" could be indefinitely committed to a mental hospital for treatment until he was certified as "cured" of his sexual psychopathology, or in the cases of the Sioux City gay men, "cured" of their homosexuality.

Daring to Dissent

Into this roiling froth of political paranoia, intense xenophobia, fear of difference, and media hysteria over the supposed dangers posed by homosexuality, gay men like Harry Hay and Rudi Gernreich asserted their voices, publicly rejecting the prescribed life of shame and secrecy for homosexuals. Popular culture and the popular news media portrayed gay men as psychopathic monsters preying upon innocent children. The president of the United States had declared them unfit for public service, and countless gay and lesbian public employees lost their jobs. And yet Hay and the members of the Mattachine Society dared to dissent and to imagine a world in which their homosexuality would not be automatic disqualification from dignity, decency, and the fundamental rights of citizenship. Mattachine and its sister organization, the Daughters of Bilitis, carved out safe harbor for the women and men who refused to live in shame and those groups began the slow work of building confidence among themselves so that public challenges to homophobia could be mounted. One important success of Mattachine's came in 1952 when the group forced Los Angeles police to drop charges against a Mattachine member who had been entrapped in a sex sting operation.

But even while these tiny organizations pursued their modest immediate goal of safe social space and respite from an unrelenting political, legal, and cultural assault on their humanity, the suspicion of gay people as disloyal traitors dogged Mattachine's leadership. Harry Hay, himself a former member of the Communist Party, was driven out of Mattachine in a brutally effective purge of its leftist founders. Mattachine's new leaders took the organization in a decidedly more conservative direction, choosing to build alliances with medical professionals and psychiatrists in hopes that these surrogates would advocate for more fair treatment of gay people. But a large obstacle blocked that route to social equality: the American Psychiatric Association had classified homosexuality as a mental illness. The very same professionals to whom Mattachine's new leadership looked for affirmation and support described them as mentally ill, in need of medical treatment for their pathology.

To the Streets, to the Halls of Power

The apparently intractable institutional homophobia, as expressed in the APA classification of homosexuality as a disease, that faced early LGBT organizers would be challenged in the decades that followed. But a more determined and more militant style of LGBT organizing would be required. For that, our movement must thank Franklin Kameny, an astrophysicist who in 1957 had been fired from his job in the U.S. government after an arrest on public loitering charges, a violation frequently brought against openly gay men who dared to be seen in public spaces. Kameny commenced a decades-long battle that ultimately led to a 1975 rescission of civil service rules barring homosexuals from employment. Although Kameny never regained his job with the government, he found a new calling as an activist for the rights of openly LGBT people to work, live, and love. Kameny, with others in the Washington, D.C., area, founded a local Mattachine chapter in 1961. He was elected its leader and brought the most forceful and publicly visible program of political activities to bear upon institutional homophobia. Kameny and his organization engaged for the first time ever in public demonstrations to demand fair treatment for homosexuals from the federal government. Kameny, doing what no one had dared do before, led a group of women and men in public protests at the White House and at the Liberty Bell site in Philadelphia in 1965. He refused to tremble before the institutions of homosexual oppression and, in so doing, he inspired millions of others to stand up for themselves. Kameny is credited with coining the seminal phrase "gay is good," echoing in sentiment and message another catchphrase of the 1960s, "black is beautiful."

But even Kameny, who boldly asserted the goodness of gayness, remained aware of the public image of homosexuals. The women and men who demonstrated in front of the White House observed a dress code: men in shirts and ties and women in dresses. These were not the drag queens and butch dykes and scruffy, unkempt people who would, four years later, fight the New York City cops in street battles outside the Stonewall Inn. These were professional women and men, demanding fair treatment but staying within bounds of heterosexually defined

decorum. Twenty-two years after the landmark demonstrations led by
Frank Kameny, I was excoriated by Kameny himself at a public forum
on sodomy-law repeal for urging that arguments against sodomy laws
needed to address not only privacy concerns but also the right of a people to freely engage in sexual relations, and that our failure to demand
sexual freedom would limit the meaning and impact of our work to repeal sodomy laws.

They Don't Call Us Crazy Anymore

The rise of a new militancy among LGBT activists and organizations,
as evidenced by Kameny's decades-long and successful struggle to top-
ple the U.S. Civil Service rules that cost him his career, strengthened
challenges to the most formidable aspects of institutional homophobia.
With respect to the ways in which homosexuality was understood, both
by elites and by ordinary people, our movement's most important task
would be to challenge and change the classification of homosexuality
as a mental illness. The American Psychiatric Association's *Diagnostic
and Statistical Manual of Mental Disorders* (DSM) in 1952 codified homosexuality as a "sociopathic personality disorder" to be treated and
cured through medical and scientific means. The DSM classification
was the theoretical infrastructure supporting sexual-psychopath laws at
the state level, the federal government's immigration rules excluding
openly homosexual people from entering the country, the incarceration
of countless homosexuals in public and private mental institutions,
and the medical torture and torment of gay people by shock therapy,
aversion therapy, electroshock therapy, castration, and lobotomy. The
legacy of understanding homosexuality as a mental disorder still echoes
in contemporary society through the practice of conversion or repar-
ative therapy and LGBT "deprogramming" centers run by quasi-
professional practitioners who claim that homosexuality can be cured
or simply rejected by individuals whose force of will is buttressed by a
relationship with a deity or higher power. Contemporary political lead-

ers such as Senator Trent Lott of Mississippi unabashedly equate ho-mosexuality with addictions commonly understood to be diseases or behavioral disorders. "It is [a sin].... You should try to show them a way to deal with that problem, just like alcohol...or sex addiction... or kleptomaniacs," said Lott, as quoted by the Associated Press on June 15, 1998, during his term as majority leader of the United States Senate.

Much like the struggle to win sodomy repeal by working with the American Law Institute, activists targeted the American Psychiatric Association classification in order to change the attitudes and practices of an elite opinion-setting professional body. On December 15, 1973, activists scored a huge victory when the APA declassified homosexuality, one that reverberated throughout the psychiatric community and the medical care system and then, through the legal, lawmaking, media, and educational institutions of the country. Declassification brought lasting and durable change to the way homosexuality was understood, described, and regarded by elites, which in turn trickled down and filtered out through American society. Despite opinions that still emanate from fringe groups like the National Association for Research and Therapy of Homosexuality, an organization that promotes the disease/disorder model of homosexuality, and the discredited Nebraska psychologist Paul Cameron, who made a career of associating homosexuals with murder and child abuse, and extremist politicians like Trent Lott, "sociopath" has been permanently removed from the defamatory weapons wielded against us by anti-LGBT leaders and organizations. Reasonable leaders and reasonable people, no matter how they view homosexuality, simply can't, don't, and won't call us crazy anymore. The established professional organizations of psychiatry, psychology, and social work consistently and publicly declare that homosexuality, in and of itself, does not constitute mental ill health, perhaps the single greatest achievement of the LGBT movement for social change. As well, the professional organizations of the mental health fields speak out time and again to advocate for the complete and full equality of LGBT people in American society.

The title of this section, "They Don't Call Us Crazy Anymore," might more accurately be stated as, "When They Call Us Crazy, They Get Called On It." The Associated Press reported on June 20, 2006, that a government document, a "Defense Department Instruction," lists homosexuality alongside mental retardation and personality disorders among the department's grounds for discharge from the armed services. The Center for the Study of Sexual Minorities in the Military, at the University of California at Santa Barbara, uncovered the document. A statement issued by James H. Scully Jr., president of the American Psychiatric Association, made clear the APA's view on this topic, now more than three decades old: "Based on scientific and medical evidence, the APA declassified homosexuality as a mental disorder in 1973—a position shared by all other major health and mental health organizations based on their own review of science." According to the Associated Press, nine members of Congress, in a June 19 letter to the secretary of defense, demanded a review of all Pentagon documents and policies to ensure that homosexuality is no longer included on any lists of psychological disorders.

Communities and Community Images

The legacy of labels of criminality, sexual psychopathology, and perversion can be seen in both historical and contemporary political debates about LGBT people. In the 1970s Anita Bryant and her husband, Bob Green, early leaders of the emerging politicized religious right wing, became the architects of the first wave of antigay ballot initiatives to repeal hard-won laws banning discrimination against gay people. Bryant and Green amplified popular culture's image of gay people as dangerous. During a 1977 campaign in Miami/Dade County, Florida, to repeal a newly passed nondiscrimination law, Bryant frequently made the following point: "Homosexuals cannot reproduce—so they must recruit. And to freshen their ranks, they must recruit the youth of America."

The image of gay endangerment of children is still deployed against us by those seeking to deny our basic rights. In contemporary discussions of same-sex marriage and adoption of children by LGBT parents, the gay predator lurks on the edge of the public debate, sometimes taking center stage. As recently as February 25, 2006, Republican state representative Debra Maggart of Tennessee declared in a letter to a constituent published in *Out & About* newspaper in Nashville, "We also have seen evidence that homosexual couples prey on young males and have, in some instances, adopted them in order to have unfettered access to subject them to a life of molestation and sexual abuse." The leadership of the Roman Catholic Church drew upon similar fears when they claimed, in a July 2003 Vatican statement on same-sex unions (*Considerations Regarding Proposals to Give Legal Recognition to Unions between Homosexual Persons*), that placing children into same-sex households was "gravely immoral" and "would actually mean doing violence to these children." Although the Vatican's language is somewhat more circumspect than Anita Bryant's or Representative Maggart's, the message is clear: gay people commit violent acts against innocent children.

While our movement has forcefully and successfully refuted the categorical smears of criminality of adult sexuality and mental illness, when confronted with descriptions of gay and lesbian people as dangerous to children, the LGBT movement's response has been confused and ambivalent. Activist leaders variously run from the topic, disavow proponents of intergenerational relationships as not part of a gay community context, craft organizing materials and events that feature only the most wholesome (i.e., acceptable to the mainstream) aspects of LGBT community, censor the more colorful characters in LGBT communities, and, most recently, heavily promote our own population of gay- and lesbian-headed families, as well as LGBT leaders of faith. Some of these communications strategies represent the logical outcome of ever-growing and ever-diversifying LGBT communities, particularly as regards the burgeoning and increasingly visible and active LGBT families and LGBT people of faith. After all, the more of us who come out, the more different kinds of LGBT people there will be to self-identify to neighbors and coworkers and employers and the media. But other efforts to neutralize homosexuality and transgenderism and bisexuality seem strained and marked by the kind of social embarrassment caused when family members are not presentable to outsiders.

The annual hand-wringing in many cities across the country over media representations of pride events is one example of an ongoing conversation within LGBT circles over how we look to ourselves and to the mainstream general public. LGBT newspapers become the community forum for a now-routine debate about the local mainstream media's choices of photos in pride coverage when media depictions focus on LGBT sexual subcultures. Writers of letters to the editors often describe drag queens, dykes on bikes, butches, femmes, and transgender people, gym bunnies decorating floats in their jock straps, as too outré for daytime, all-ages public events. The protestations about sisters and brothers who are not-ready-for-daytime-exposure usually reprise a vigorous debate that has been ongoing since the 1980s at least, one that casts some LGBT people as vampire-like figures only suitable for forays into public spaces when darkness has fallen and the good people are tucked safely away.

This anxious intracommunity discussion can be understood in the context of a history of popular association of homosexuality with crime, sexual predation, perversity, and untrustworthiness. Our sexual and gender subcultures produce all manner of rebellion, transgression, and resistance to social authorities and expectations. The question is this: Is the movement goal of securing full equality under the law jeopardized by our communities' traditional allegiance to a flourishing and rebellious subculture? Is the public relations battle lost when the more outrageous members of our LGBT family are seen, heard, and identified beyond our ghetto boundaries? How many "good gays" does it take to refute the slanderous hangovers from the bad old days of sexual-psychopathic ideologies, and is it worth the effort to do so? What do we really gain and lose by disassociating ourselves from sisters and brothers whose queerness will never fit into a corporate suit?

No Dress Code for Civil Rights, Human Dignity, and Social Justice

In a book published in 1989, *After the Ball: How America Will Conquer Its Fear and Hatred of Gays in the 90s,* by Marshall Kirk and Hunter Madsen, the authors argued that in order to win our political battles, the LGBT movement should seek to promote white and middle-class gays living lives indistinguishable from those of typical suburbanites. The authors framed the debate in almost irresistible and pragmatic terms: If we want to win our civil rights, this is what we must and should do.

In the movement that matured in response to the AIDS crisis, our organizations grew in strength, capacities, and budgets. AIDS delivered one unifying message to LGBT people: our very survival depended on our willingness to build and deploy political power in the struggle to gain access to government dollars for desperate and needy community-based AIDS-service organizations all over the country. Our organizations responded with determination and fierceness; public and private money began to flow to the service and care agencies assisting people with AIDS. Money and power attracted powerful and hard-charging leadership as the communities' AIDS health crisis deepened and widened. Leaders and potential leaders migrated from corporate and institutional entities into the AIDS and LGBT organizations. Inevitably, a preponderance of new leaders were white gay men who had been shaken from their comfortable pursuits of career success by the epidemic ravaging the lives of friends and loved ones. This new cadre of leaders brought with them into our movement the attitudes and values of business professionalism, remaking the movement to be politically stronger, more firmly established, and more respectable in the eyes of funders, major donors, and political allies.

The trajectory from "mom and pop" (or pop and pop/mom and mom) styles of organizing and organizational structure to service agency/corporate models created consternation and alienation among more leftist, intellectual, and countercultural grassroots thinkers and leaders. In their critique of the LGBT movement of the 1990s, led by publishers of the now-defunct *Gay Community News* in Boston and

Out/Look magazine in San Francisco, writers challenged the corporatization of the movement, its striving for both hegemony and mainstream tolerance, its reformist goals and its apparent embarrassment about the sexual subcultures of LGBT communities. In one famous episode, movement founder Harry Hay rebelled against the organizers of the 1986 Los Angeles Pride Parade, who banned a contingent of the North American Man/Boy Love Association from marching. Hay, in his inimitable style, marched solo bearing a sign that read: "NAMBLA walks with me." The 1993 March on Washington was criticized for focusing media attention on the plight of openly LGB servicemembers in the armed forces. March organizers were later accused of disinviting retired U.S. Army Sergeant Perry Watkins, the only dishonorably discharged gay servicemember to have won a legal case for back pay and honorable discharge from the army, because Watkins publicly acknowledged his drag performances and sexual relations with commissioned officers while still in uniform. I heard Watkins tell a raucously funny and ironic story about his reputation for "giving the best blow jobs" on his base when he spoke at the 1989 Creating Change Conference in Alexandria, Virginia. But Perry Watkins was evidently deemed too black, too queer, too outrageous, and too difficult to explain to straight allies.

The catch-22 of the "positive portrayal" strategy is this: Our political adversaries of the anti-LGBT right-wing movements have access to the same photos of drag queens, leather boys and girls, and gym bunnies on pride floats as do we. The right-wing organizations harvest and then use these very same images to paint a monolithic picture of our communities: perverse, depraved, gender disoriented, and sexually obsessed, all of which means dangerous under their terms. One infamous propaganda film of the right-wing, *The Gay Agenda,* produced by the Christian Action Network in 1992, puts on full display our adversaries' eagerness to selectively deploy outré images of LGBT people in order to illustrate the alleged threat of homosexual people to their social order. *The Gay Agenda* circulated to great effect in the states of Colorado and Oregon during anti-LGBT ballot-question campaigns in the early

1990s, when Colorado voters enacted the first and most draconian of all the constitutional amendments to limit the citizenship rights of LGBT people. Amendment 2, as it was known, was struck down by the U.S. Supreme Court in 1996 with the simple but pointed observation that citizens cannot be made "strangers to the law" on the basis of animus, or contempt, directed at them by other citizens.

Our political movement and its leaders, representing our many and diverse communities, cannot wield a centralizing and consolidating authority over all aspects of LGBT expressive life. So no matter how awkward it may be, for those of us who lobby in the legislatures and appear on news programs, that the vampires among us walk the streets by day as well as by night, it is simply who we are as a collection of communities. Political advocates for any cause invariably attempt to filter out information that isn't helpful with key decision makers. After all, their jobs call on them to positively influence those who make law and social policy. But movement leaders and policy experts must guard against acting as sexual cleansers; we cannot, in the end, collude and cooperate with an ideology that pursues a goal of queer invisibility. The political movement cannot be the enforcer of a dress code for civil rights, human dignity, and social justice, in the vain hope that our enemies will not notice drag, S and M, transgender people, bisexuals, or polyamorous perversity. At the same time, our friends and colleagues who live, work, and thrive within the LGBT sexual subcultures need to understand that a successful political strategy to pass legislation may not be affirming and satisfying as regards matters of full representation and visibility of the many and various ways we express our desires and sexualities.

The "gay" movement's embrace of bisexual and transgender people stands as a benchmark of a determination to defend sexual and gender freedom. Beginning in the mid-1990s, under the leadership of then–executive director Kerry Lobel, the National Gay and Lesbian Task Force expanded its political vision and mission to include the aspirations and political agendas of bisexual and transgender people. Lobel, who cut her political teeth in the feminist domestic-violence movement, saw keenly and clearly that our bisexual and transgender sisters and brothers are our canaries in the political coal mines. When the most obvious queers who are the least able to conceal their queernesses become prime targets for social hostilities, whether from dominant heterosexual power centers or from gay and lesbian people themselves, then none of us, not even the least noticeable lesbian soccer moms and corporate gay managers, can think of ourselves as safe from homophobic harm. The sexual and gender freedom for bisexual and transgender people is all of our sexual and gender freedoms. Lobel turned her considerable energies, acumen, and personal charm to the goal of building a movement that would be welcoming to Sgt. Perry Watkins; Bangor, Maine, gay-bashing victim and femme gay man Charles Howard; and Newark, New Jersey, lesbian-bashing victim Sakia Gunn. As an observant Jew and a woman, Lobel said in numerous public speeches, "I will not leave any part of myself outside the doors of this movement. I will ask no other person to leave any part of him or herself outside the doors of this movement." After nearly a decade of internal debate and countless refusals to acknowledge the place of bisexual people and transgender people in a movement of sexual and gender minorities, Lobel opened the door to the canaries in the mine and pledged to honor, support, and work for and with an inclusive movement for freedom, equality, and justice.

There is another, and more personal, way that internal sexual cleansing in the movement backfires on our leadership. Some leaders of LGBT organizations participate in the lively sexual subcultures in our communities. The right wing has, from time to time, surfaced information about the sexual lives of LGBT leaders and attempted to use it to discredit them, their organizations, and the movement. Right-wing opponents of LGBT people regularly identified Peri Jude Radecic, the executive director of the National Gay and Lesbian Task Force in the early 1990s, as a leather dyke. Had she not been out and proud of her own positioning in sexual subcultures, this exposure by right-wing activists could have been a potent tactic against Radecic and the organization. But Radecic spoke publicly about being part of the LGBT leather community and would not be intimidated by her enemies. Just like the movement founders who had flung open their closet doors to reject shame and claim their homosexuality, Radecic had flung open her own closet to claim her sexual desires and act on them. Not only was her leather identity not a skeleton in her closet, she didn't even own a sexuality closet that right-wing enemies could raid.

GAME PLAN FOR CHAPTER THREE
Sexual-Psychopath Laws

The sexual-psychopath laws, especially those enacted during the McCarthy-era witch hunts against homosexuals, were used as tools of persecution of gay men. Currently, sexual-offender laws and social policies are typically engaged to identify and cope with the social problems of rape, sexual abuse and exploitation of children, sexual violence, and antisocial predatory behaviors. While broad support for these laws emanates from a desire to protect children from sexual exploitation, they are often so broadly written, in many instances they have been used to prosecute gay male consensual sexual activity. The particular histories of persecutions of gay men, whose lives were disrupted and sometimes destroyed when they were committed to mental institutions and subjected to medical "cures" for homosexuality, highlight an especially dark and dangerous chapter in our communities and our movement. By entering "LGBT and sexual-psychopath laws" and "1950s gay witch hunts" into your search engine, you can find links to articles that detail many instances of government and police crackdowns on gay men.

Media Watchdog

The Gay & Lesbian Alliance against Defamation (GLAAD) is the only national LGBT organization that monitors and critiques the way LGBT people are portrayed by the media. GLAAD has worked with both news outlets and the entertainment industry to eliminate bias in images of LGBT people and communities. Founded in 1985, GLAAD formed when the New York Post, a large daily paper in New York City, presented sensational and defamatory accounts of the AIDS/HIV epidemic and gay men. In 1987 GLAAD successfully advocated for the *New York Times*, the country's newspaper of record, to change its editorial policy to use the word "gay," rather than "homosexual." Since then, GLAAD has spearheaded many other advocacy campaigns to rid media of both bias and invisibility of LGBT people. For example, GLAAD secured a policy change at Hallmark Cards when the company took the word "lesbian" off its list of banned words. From the seemingly mundane use of language in mass-produced greeting cards to the more profound challenges of on-air homophobic commentaries and uses of slurs, GLAAD has maintained a watchful eye on mainstream media. Visit the group's Web site to learn more about GLAAD's ongoing work to promote and ensure "fair, accurate and inclusive representation of people and events in the media as a means of eliminating homophobia and discrimination based on gender identity and sexual orientation."

Try This at Home: Respond to Coverage of LGBT People in the Media

In American society, free speech is guaranteed in the Bill of Rights of the U.S. Constitution. Responding to media coverage of LGBT people and issues offers us a way to use our freedom of speech so that we have an effect on how producers of media images and consumers of media images think about us. Our interactions with media producers—i.e., reporters, editors, photographers, and publishers—should be framed by an appreciation for free speech and free expression of ideas and not with a goal of censoring speech. Our goal in responding to negative media portrayals or invisibility will be to correct the record and present a more accurate picture of LGBT people.

When covering LGBT people and issues, especially in the heated political contemporary debates over outlawing forms of discrimination like arbitrary firings of LGBT people, the media frequently seeks out our opponents for an "opposing view." Media representatives defend this practice by claiming that they are obligated to present a "balanced" view of the issue. But when the opposing viewpoint is reliant on homophobic stereotypes or religious condemnations of LGBT people, it's time to take action. Here are some guidelines for monitoring and responding to media portrayals of our communities.

- *Read, listen, watch.* We need to pay attention to how we are presented and discussed in the media. Make it a daily habit to read a general readership newspaper, a community newspaper of special interest to you, or to watch/listen to news programming on television or the radio.
- *Observe how LGBT people are described.* Are words or images neutral in description or presentation? Are we referred to as "avowed" or "admitted" LGBT people, or as "openly" LGBT people. Do we have lives, or a "lifestyle"? Does our movement advocate for changes in law, or do we promote a "homosexual agenda"? Are we seeking participation in our communities, or are we "taking over"? Do we "flaunt" our sexuality, or are we expressing our love/affection for our partners?
- *Evaluate the words used to characterize LGBT people as compared with words describing other people.* Would a person or group of people from any other identified minority be similarly described? Do people of Jewish faith "avow" their Jewishness? Is there a "lifestyle" ascribed to any other group of people you can name? Are leaders from other social justice movements said to have an overarching "agenda"? Do heterosexual couples who engage in affectionate touching in public "flaunt" their sexuality? Are billboards featuring photographs of straight people touching each other said to be for the purpose of recruiting young people into a life of heterosexuality, or simply to advertise products?
- *Respond to what you read, see, and hear.* When you notice that LGBT people are described with words or images that seem to be chosen especially to appeal to anti-LGBT sentiments, respond directly to the media outlet.
- *Go directly to the source of the anti-LGBT bias.* Begin with the person who is identified as being responsible for the article or segment of the show, in other words, the reporter, the newscaster,

or the news producer. Interacting with print reporters is typically straightforward. In this age of electronic communications, reporters e-mail addresses often appear at the end of their stories or opinion columns. Television and radio reporters sometimes, but not always, generate their own stories and reports, so additional research about who actually writes the stories may be required. Most reputable news outlets encourage reporters to interact with readers, viewers, and listeners.

• *Be direct and specific.* Reference the article or report and quote as accurately as you can from the report itself. Be clear and specific about what you want to correct and then do so. Promise to read and listen carefully in the future to assess whether your feedback has had an impact.

• *Communicate with the editor of the publication or news program.* If the reporter or newscaster refuses to engage with you, write a letter to the editor for publication in the paper; or write directly to the producer of an electronic news program. Be brief, be specific, and clearly state how the article or show fell short of your expectations for unbiased news coverage.

• *Take your criticisms to a "readers' advocate" or community liaison.* If the bias you identified continues to appear in the paper or radio or television broadcast, bring it to the attention of an ombudsman. Most large media operations dedicate a staff person to interacting with readers and listeners.

• *Contact the editor-in-chief or general manager.* If the previous steps bring no positive change, the next stop in the organizational chain of command is the editor-in-chief of a paper or the general manager of a TV or radio station. Request an in-person meeting for you and a few other community advocates. Prepare for the meeting by finding examples of the kind of coverage you think is biased. Be brief, specific, and clear about how the coverage is hurtful to you and to the community. Be specific about how the news outlet can do a better job. Promise to continue to read, watch, and listen for a change in reporting about LGBT people, issues, and community.

• *Don't give up.* Efforts to effect change in media coverage may get immediate results, but sometimes making a difference takes a persistent effort by a group of dedicated advocates. So don't be discouraged. Positive change in media coverage affects thousands and thousands of other people.

Sample Letter to the Editor

Dear Editor,

Your article about efforts to pass a nondiscrimination law by the City Council ("Anti-Bias Proposal Raises Temperatures in City," September 30, 2006) included a quotation from Rev. John Johnson of Traditional Family Values. Johnson said, "Homosexuals live a decadent lifestyle. Their chosen path to damnation doesn't deserve approval by the rest of us." Johnson's use of the phrase "decadent lifestyle" insults all of us who need the nondiscrimination bill to keep our jobs and our homes. I don't have a "decadent lifestyle." Like my neighbors, I live in a modest home with my partner. The last bit of "decadence" I recall was the purchase of a pint of premium ice cream. We both work to support our family and we need to know that we won't lose our jobs because we are gay. I don't believe I am on a path to damnation by living in an honest way, true to who I am, and I don't need Johnson's approval. He can hold whatever opinions he wants about gay people, but those opinions don't belong in an article about ending arbitrary bias in employment and housing. His inflammatory condemnations of me and other gay people have no place in rational discussions about employment discrimination in our city. If there is a sound reason to oppose the nondiscrimination bill, I'd like to hear it. It certainly isn't coming from Johnson.

Sincerely,
Joe Doe
123 Elm Avenue
Elmwood, USA

4

Tools of Our Trade

Changing the world to secure full equality, human dignity, and sexual and gender freedom for LGBT people requires patience, perseverance, and great faith in one another and in the capacity of human beings to transform their thinking about sexuality and gender difference. It also requires tools, tactics, energy, and the relentless pursuit of concrete goals, one at a time. One at a time. Dramatic and earthshaking achievements like the American Psychiatric Association's declassification of homosexuality as a disease represent exceptional and decisive highwater marks of our movement's ongoing work; more typically, our steps in LGBT progress are much smaller and our achievements more modest. But taken all together, these small and modest steps lead inexorably to equality, dignity, and freedom.

The recipe for our hard-won victories calls for great quantities of community building, grassroots mobilizing, advocacy, lobbying, and communications and public education. These ingredients can be applied in a rational way that results in political wins to bring about change to major institutions, which then turn the lever of social change. By winning the seemingly small political victories, the LGBT movement cumulatively builds an ever-expanding record of both public and private institutional recognition of LGBT people as students and teachers, employees and employers, citizens and voters, worshippers, taxpayers, family members, soldiers and sailors, athletes, artists, workers, and consumers.

While our movement forebears and founders concerned themselves with the two foundational goals of creating safe harbor for LGBT people and eliminating governmental hostilities to our sexual and gender choices, the contemporary LGBT political movement seeks more than governmental neutrality. We want and need the powers of government at all levels to recognize and defend our basic human right to pursue life, liberty, and happiness. Freedom from fear and harm still must be won for many of us; but for all of us, a common understanding of LGBT people as full human beings and citizens must be secured.

In the United States, all levels of government serve a central purpose of articulating in concrete practices and policies who is included in the definition of citizen and how the rights and responsibilities of citizens will be defined, protected, and defended. Governments, for lack of a better image, are bundles of resources deployed in our collective interests and for our collective benefit. When any group of people is categorically excluded from significant and central institutions of government, the impact of exclusion reverberates throughout the communities of the excluded group. For example, although we assert that LGBT people deserve full citizenship, when we are categorically disallowed from serving in the U.S. Armed Forces, the singularly qualifying quid pro quo of defending homeland in exchange for citizenship rights is simply unavailable to us. By contrast, when the U.S. Armed Forces became racially integrated in the years following World War II, during which African Americans served in large numbers, a critical barrier to dismantling codified segregation fell and the civil rights movement advocated for further expansion of civil rights, in part on the basis of the quid pro quo. Put most simply, how could African American people be denied the rights of citizenship when black men and women had fulfilled a central responsibility of citizenship: serving, fighting, and dying in World War II and subsequent conflicts?

Just as was true for women and people of color seeking full political participation, LGBT people have met the government and it is not us. It is for this reason that LGBT people engage in governmentally related projects and campaigns, including running for elective offices. The organizing of the late 1980s and early 1990s to rescind the military's ban on openly LGB servicemembers garnered much criticism from within our movement because it was seen to attach us to the very worst aspects of the status quo: the military machinery of this country and all the ugly histories of conquest and empire. After all, why would we wish to associate with the post–Cold War right-wing aspirations for world domination? But critics failed to grapple with the stark realities of the military's homophobic policies and consequent witch hunts against uniformed LGB people that still ruin lives and careers of otherwise qualified servicemembers, the majority of whom are in the enlisted ranks. If the primary purpose of our movement remains to end the prosecution, persecution, and punishment of people for their sexual orientation and/or gender expression, then we are called to challenge homophobia wherever it exists and whomever it targets. While many of the goals of our movement have to do with reform of laws, policies, and practices of government, we err if we presume that reformist goals do not themselves represent powerful shifts in how LGBT people are viewed. To move from social pariahs to full citizens is to forever alter the social and political landscape in which we live.

Altering the social and political landscape means building a powerful movement and continually expanding the numbers of people who support our goals. What follows is a brief review of some strategies to build a durable and sustainable base of support and to increase the political power in LGBT communities.

Standing Together

Campaigns and projects that raise the community's collective esteem and sense of solidarity of experiences and purpose remain central to building community. Examples of these are the thousands of LGBT pride events that annually gather several million people to commemorate the Stonewall riots and to visibly and publicly refuse shame and claim pride in our sexual and gender identities and communities. The events occur in towns and cities across the United States, from Bangor, Maine, to Johnson City, Tennessee, to Juneau, Alaska, and in every major metropolitan area. Pride events also punctuate the academic year at many college and university campuses, as well as some high school and elementary schools. Transgender people, LGBT people of color, LGBT religious/spiritual folk, leather people, big furry bears, lipstick lesbians, and gyrating gym bunnies organize pride events to appeal specifically to people who share their identities and interests.

Each of these gatherings boosts the morale and self-esteem of LGBT people and increases the fun quotient in our lives. All of these events build a sense of community and help to break individuals' feelings of isolation, aloneness, and loneliness. Overall, the pride events held around the country forge solidarity among us and contribute positively to our common purpose of political and social change, whether or not a specific political agenda is articulated or addressed. However, the pride rituals have also become targets of criticism, both from within our ranks and without. Some detractors in the LGBT community claim that pride gatherings have been rendered obsolete by our progress and are outmoded forms of exorcising remnants of a shame-filled past. Other detractors cringe at annual displays by so-called marginal or fringe LGBT people—dykes on bikes, drag queens, leather men and women—perhaps forgetting or blissfully ignoring the history of our movement, but certainly objecting to visibility on the part of the sexually obvious among us. And yet other LGBT critics call the annual pride events simply boring and same old/same old.

Right-wing adversaries latch on to the sexually flamboyant LGBT participants as dangerous influences on children, embarrassments to heterosexual residents, too wild, too loud, too queer. Occasionally, elected officials respond to the endangerment bait and deny pride organizers access to public facilities in an effort to snuff out LGBT visibility, as happened in Hillsborough County, Florida, in 2005. The Hillsborough County Commission adopted a resolution instructing that a gay-pride month display of LGBT-themed books for young readers be removed from a branch of the countywide library system, on the presumption that young readers need to be protected from exposure to homosexuality and homosexuals. Hillsborough County is home to the Tampa-area LGBT community, which erupted in a yearlong and very energetic campaign to resist the commission's blatant effort to shove them back into a closet. Although the book display was not restored, the resulting kerfuffle greatly strengthened local organizing in Tampa and provided a public issue around which LGBT people rallied.

As long as our adversaries and the just plain ignorant insist on distorting the truth of our lives, we will work to counteract anti-LGBT disinformation propaganda. In the continuing struggle for respect of LGBT people in Hillsborough County, one year after the county commission stripped libraries of pride book displays, organizers put together a reading from those very books. Called Embracing Tolerance, the public reading of the banned books both challenged the commission's view that LGBT people's lives ought not to be part of public discourse and let the commissioners know that their cleansing policy had not been forgotten. Another element of the Hillsborough County LGBT people's visibility campaign was a series of visibility actions called "mall walks," when LGBT people and allies wore LGBT-identifying shirts and held hands with loved ones while strolling through shopping malls.

Teachable Moments and Data Points

Most people, even our families and other LGBT people, need to learn about discrimination, bias violence, and homophobia. The education of both LGBT people and straight people about the extent of discrimination and the damage it does to all of us takes many forms. There have been, and unfortunately will continue to be, teachable organizing moments that occur when acts of vicious bias violence become widely known. The murders of Matthew Shepard and Billy Joe Gaither, and many others killed in anti-LGBT attacks, became touchstones for organizers in communities across the United States. Shepard's death, in particular, sparked media and public acknowledgment of the pervasiveness of bias violence and set off a round of soul-searching about strategies to reduce or eliminate bias violence. But while we are wise to seize upon teachable organizing moments to galvanize public and political support for concrete means to inoculate communities and protect LGBT people from these and other violent expressions of antigay feeling, we also can create ways to describe and explain how discrimination hurts us.

Most recently, the LGBT movement has encouraged the "telling of our stories." Through the media, in cultural presentations, and in political projects, LGBT people have stood up to bear witness to the toll that discrimination has taken. During the legislative campaigns to preserve the right of same-sex couples to marry in Massachusetts, bound notebooks of the first-person accounts of married same-sex couples were distributed to legislators. Grassroots organizers also encourage LGBT people to tell their stories to their own family members, by writing letters to newspapers, communicating directly and personally with legislators, participating in public forums to speak out about discrimination, and testifying at legislative hearings on bills and initiatives to ban discrimination.

In addition to personal anecdotes, though, we also have launched research projects to document the evidence of discrimination. Since the mid-1980s, local and statewide organizations have collected social science data from LGBT people and then used the data to support passage of nondiscrimination and hate-crimes laws and policies. These data-documentation projects answer lawmakers' need for discrimination evidence in a concrete and rational way, proving that there are LGBT people who live in their jurisdictions, some of whom have suffered from discrimination.

One example of the effectiveness of discrimination data documentation unfolded in Topeka, Kansas. In 1993 the Mayor's Task Force on Gay and Lesbian Concerns found "pervasive harassment and discrimination" in Topeka and called for government action to stop discrimination. But action on a local nondiscrimination law stalled for the next decade while Topeka's notorious antigay activist Fred Phelps (sponsor of the God Hates Fags Web site and hundreds of ugly pickets at funerals, including that of Matthew Shepard) intimidated local political leaders. In October 2003, Topeka's Equal Justice Coalition teamed up with the National Gay and Lesbian Task Force to collect and analyze discrimination data from a sample of LGBT residents. The survey results, released in November 2004, showed that 15 percent of LGBT respondents reported lost jobs because of their sexual orientation, 47 percent concealed their identities to avoid harassment or discrimination, and 41 percent had been victims of verbal or physical abuse in the workplace. On November 16, 2004, the Topeka City Council debated, and subsequently adopted, a law that outlaws antigay discrimination in city employment and paves the way for broader nondiscrimination measures. Following passage of the law, Fred Phelps and his supporters put a question on the ballot to repeal the nondiscrimination law. Topeka voters rejected Phelps's attack on the basic human rights of LGBT people, defeating the repeal initiative on March 1, 2005, by 52 percent to 48 percent.

Through a growing network of research and policy institutes, the LGBT movement has become ever more skilled and sophisticated in collecting and presenting social scientific data to demonstrate the effects of homophobia. Our social scientists have studied employment discrimination, bias violence, housing discrimination, inequities in the delivery of social services and public safety services, violence against and harassment of LGBT students and teachers in school settings, the negative psychological impact of living with the stresses of homophobia, and delivery of medical and mental health services. All the data supports the passage of laws and policies that challenge homophobic behaviors and ease discrimination.

Strong Organizations, Strong Leaders = A Strong Movement

Our movement works through its organizations. Committed individuals can do much, but groups of committed people who come together in strong and capable organizations can do more. Strong organizations need leaders, members, vision and action plans, money, and a solid base of support. Capable organizations need committed people with skills to organize and lead their members through a series of action steps to achieve their goals. The LGBT movement is comprised of thousands of organizations, from GSAs in schools, to local political groups, to statewide advocacy organizations, to national action organizations. All are necessary and all contribute to the common goal of eradicating homophobia and ending all forms of discrimination against LGBT people.

Strong and smart leaders build and guide strong and capable organizations. The LGBT movement's formal leadership-training opportunities can be found at annual movement conferences, training that focuses on work in specific topic areas like election campaigns, school-based organizing, workplace organizing, internship and fellowship programs at LGBT organizations, and in the curriculums of some colleges and universities, especially at the graduate course level.

Informal leadership-training opportunities abound, beginning with the simple step of joining an existing organization to become involved in its work. By involving ourselves in the work of an organization whose goals and mission we support, we will learn how to be reliable and responsive members, which itself builds our own leadership potential. Whether or not we choose to take on a leadership role in an organization, we can support our leaders by being reliable members of an organization and working with others for the betterment of that organization. Leaders need followers who form a base of support for the organization. Good members offer feedback and suggestions, resist personal attacks on other members or leaders, complete tasks within a reasonable time, refrain from public criticisms of the organization or its leaders but rather work within the organizational context to resolve issues, and offer time, energy, and resources to the organization to help it meets its goals.

Winning Seats at the Table

Straight allies who serve as public officials can do much to advance our goals, but there is no substitute for actually having seats at the tables of political decision-making. A very special group of LGBT leaders are the members of our community who step forward to run for public offices, like city councils or state legislatures or state and national offices, such as governor, congressperson, or the president. (At present, no openly LGBT person has run for governor of a state or for the presidency, but it will happen someday.) Of the five hundred thousand or so public elected officials in the United States, fewer than five hundred are openly LGBT people. These men and women put themselves squarely in the public eye to advocate on behalf of the rest of us. Each of them must also appeal to a majority of the voters in their districts, which means that their agendas, or platforms, must address issues that go far beyond the specific needs and interests of their LGBT constituents.

The Democratic congresspeople Barney Frank of Massachusetts and Tammy Baldwin of Wisconsin regularly advocate at the federal level for a host of LGBT issues, while also applying themselves in other arenas, such as the economic health of the nation, health care financing, education, national security, and protections of civil liberties. Regardless of how high or low the office being sought by a candidate who is LGBT, a successful candidate, and officeholder, reaches out to voters by offering solutions to problems that are common to many people. As voters ourselves, LGBT people may support LGBT candidates both because we believe they will advocate for LGBT issues and because we support their stands on a broader range of issues. Conversely, some LGBT voters will decline to support LGBT candidates when issues outside our communities become paramount.

The sexual orientation/gender identity of LGBT candidates at some point becomes a campaign issue, but if our candidates are to survive and thrive in office, that issue likely needs to be neutralized or fade into background information about the candidate. This dynamic can seem contradictory at first. After all, we want out and proud LGBT candidates to run for and win elected offices so that the concerns of our communities are represented in lawmaking contexts. But we also must remember that elected officials' jobs call on them to represent all of their constituents. Otherwise, they will not be able to keep their jobs and we lose strong advocates with high public profiles.

A Movement For and Of All of Us

Within the LGBT movement, there is perhaps no more important and thorny problem than that of building a movement that represents all members of our communities. The young and the old. LGBT people of all races and colors and ethnicities. Bisexual and transgender people, as well as lesbians and gay men. LGBT people who are living with physical disabilities and challenges. The secular and the spiritual/religious. The working class, the poor, the middle class, and the wealthy. LGBT people come in every shape, size, and from every cultural sector of our complicated society.

We are everywhere and we are everyone and within this statement of fact can be found both blessing and challenge. It is a blessing because when we come out, we come from every part of the United States and every cultural community of origin and we can engage and educate families, friends, and neighbors who share our point of origin. It is a challenge because our diversity means that there can never be a fully representative movement that is also monolithically uniform in its makeup. The LGBT movement transforms itself constantly to understand and include LGBT people of all kinds. But the process of transformation can be a painful one and lead to alienation and mistrust. Historically, our movement has been predominantly gay, white, male, and middle class. After much struggle through the 1970s and 1980s, lesbians emerged with strong demands to be included, creating a lesbian and gay movement. After more struggle in the 1990s, bisexual and transgender people also emerged with strong demands to be included, creating a lesbian, gay, bisexual, and transgender movement.

While these efforts at building a movement that is co-gender and inclusive of bisexual people and transgender and gender-variant people are hardly finished, certainly we have had much greater success with this process than that of building a movement inclusive of LGBT people of color, immigrants, and working-class and poor people. A central obstacle to building a multiracial and multiclass movement remains the movement's own history of white and middle-/upper-class control of the resources and the agenda for LGBT organizing. Autonomous organizing by people of color and working-class/poor people both builds community and solidarity among LGBTs who share very specific life experiences and cultural contexts, and compels white-dominated organizations to engage in peer-to-peer working relationships with the organizations by, for, and about people of color and working-class and poor people. While working-class/poor LGBT organizing exists in only a few cities, there are autonomous groups by, for, and about LGBT people of color in every major urban area in the country, as well as national organizations of African American, Latino/a, Asian American, and Native American lesbians, gays, bisexual, and transgender people. At some personal cost to themselves, some LGBT people of color choose to work within predominantly white contexts. It is clear that the energies and presence of colleagues of color make a difference in how some white-dominated organizations set their agendas, use their resources to support causes of importance to communities of color, and support the leadership development of people of color. However, the internal pressure that LGBT people of color exert to influence the decisions and choices of white-dominated groups is greatly augmented by the external pressure applied by people-of-color-dominated peer organizations.

Autonomous organizing by LGBTs of color strengthens our movement in other ways. For example, in the struggle over same-sex marriage, right-wing opponents have successfully mobilized some high-profile community leaders of color to stand against us, particularly ministerial leaders of important congregations. In this instance especially, but in other issues as well, the vital advocacy roles played by LGBT organizations by, for, and about people of color become amplified. White-dominated LGBT groups can have only limited sway over the political positioning of these influential leaders of color. But LGBT people of color and their organizations enter these intracommunity debates with immediate standing in their communities of origin. When they tell their stories and advocate for the right to marry, they have the credibility of common life experience with their audiences. It is in all of our interests to sustain and value autonomous organizing of LGBT people of color, and further, to ensure that LGBT organizers working within their cultural communities of origin receive a full measure of respect for their work.

Meaningful Victories Make Durable Change

Talk is cheap. A multitude of good ideas about moving our freedom and equality agenda forward yields nothing unless some of the ideas are framed as action items with achievable outcomes. In every organizing context, we pose the questions: What do we want? Why do we want it? How are we going to get it?

For example, students and other campus activists at colleges and universities have recognized that gender-specific restrooms pose a real-life problem for transgender and gender-variant people. Recognizing this, they describe, first to themselves and then to one another, transgender and gender-variant people's daily experiences of invisibility, physical vulnerability to violence and harassment from other restroom users, and anxiety and tension generated by the constant confrontation of compulsory male/female identities that are displayed on the doors of gender-specific restrooms. A next step is to identify potential allies by expanding the universe of restroom users who might welcome gender-neutral bathrooms: mothers who must escort a young son into a restroom, fathers who must escort a young daughter, and parents of intersex children who simply don't know how to safely guide their child into the "right" restroom. As well, women and men who feel no particular threat in the concept of using common restrooms can be called on for support. Making the case to one another is an important precursor to making the case to decision makers. But the decision makers come next. Who is in charge of the restrooms at the school? Every college and university dedicates administrators and staff to facilities management and operations: the toilet paper stops at those desks. Other important action steps could include passing resolutions in the schools' LGBT organizations, student government, and faculty government, and, if necessary, collecting testimonials from people whose health and safety depend on access to gender-free restrooms. Supportive articles and editorials can be sought in campus publications. Buttons or easily applied stickers with catchy slogans can be distributed, showing a wide range of support. Petitions to the administration can be circulated. The case must be made to the decision makers and, if necessary, to the campus community at large. Persistence and determination must be applied to the project, since the case may need to be made repeatedly and to different groups of opinion makers until a consensus is built that gender-neutral restrooms will be designated on campus.

The formula for success:

Concrete goal + action plan + solid message + building and showing support + precision targeting of administrators of primary responsibility + persistence = success!

Change Means Making Choices

Organizing within the American political system presents activists and organizers with a complicated set of choices and problems, but also an amazing range of potential achievements. A quick review of victories for LGBT people shows that we have passed antidiscrimination laws in seventeen states; nine of these laws include protections for transgender people. Twenty-nine states and the District of Columbia have hate-crimes statutes that specifically cover violent crimes motivated by the real or perceived sexual orientation of the victim; the laws of seven of those states and the District of Columbia include crimes motivated by gender identity. Nearly three hundred cities, counties, or government organizations provide some level of protection against employment discrimination based on sexual orientation, and a small but growing number include gender expression. Nearly two thousand gay-straight alliances in schools all across the United States offer support for LGBT and questioning youth as well as straight allies. As this text is being written, we pour movement energy into challenges to the military exclusion of LGB people and to discriminatory marriage laws.

Successful political organizing rests on two critical themes: With whom do we work? And how do we speak to them? The answer to the first is twofold: Organizers work with a complex network of interconnected and overlapping points of influence, elected leaders being the most obvious, but also including other opinion leaders like the media and civic/religious leaders and personal networks that include family, friends, and coworkers. We also apply direct and indirect pressure on large elected or appointed decision-making bodies, such as governmental executive branches, legislatures, and the courts. Effective interactions with individuals or groups require choosing the best way to communicate and the most persuasive arguments to engage their understanding and to win their support. Having at the ready a full menu of methods of communication and points of persuasion is vital.

Tactical options that LGBT people use in fighting for equality under the law are briefly discussed below.

Hitting the Streets

Street-level demonstrations raise the visibility of a particular issue in the larger community. This tactic is especially useful if an issue has not yet gained any traction with the media and is relatively unnoticed by the general public and decision makers. In the earliest days of the AIDS epidemic, the activist group ACT UP staged countless public demonstrations to bring to everyone's attention the terrible scourge of the epidemic and its toll on gay men. These demonstrations persisted and grew in size, scope, scale, and intensity until mainstream media, governmental agencies, health care providers, and drug researchers and manufacturers took seriously the largest public health emergency of the past fifty years.

Public demonstrations can also be a source of energy to an organization or the movement at large. Each of the four LGBT marches on

Washington, held in 1979, 1987, 1993, and 2000, has gathered hundreds of thousands of LGBT people for a weekend to articulate the needs and political demands of our movement in the nation's capital. The first three marches especially sent LGBT people back to their home communities charged up and ready to get to the work of organizing where they live and work. Similarly, a demonstration can build commitment and rally people's energies for the fight, no matter the issue. Early in the development of a key issue, and at major milestones of both victory and defeat, a rousing demonstration raises spirits and creates feelings of solidarity.

Teach, Learn, Organize

In-community educational forums create opportunities for peer-to-peer education on important issues. These can be especially important if the community faces a complicated or very new issue. During campus-based organizing to end the Vietnam War in the 1960s and 1970s, teach-ins about the war and how to stop it enthralled students, so much so that scheduled classes were sometimes abandoned for political education and organizing sessions. Community forums give both experts and organizational leaders the time and space to explain the terms of an issue, lay out an action plan, recruit others to help with the work, take feedback from members of the community, and answer questions. Important organizing work, like circulating a sign-in list or forming committees to take on specific projects, can be accomplished at community educational events.

Taking It to Our Opponents

High-decibel and spectacular confrontations with political leaders who staunchly and stubbornly oppose us bring attention to the opposition's positions and give us the opportunity to shape and control some of the public debate. When North Carolina's Senator Jesse Helms vigorously opposed AIDS-prevention efforts that included distribution of condoms, members of ACT UP dropped a huge latex condom over his home. While the senators' neighbors and supporters probably frowned on this, ACT UP's audaciousness brought its members into direct contact with the media in Helms's hometown of Raleigh and his home state of North Carolina. ACT UP dominated the media, explaining that Helms opposed necessary and life-saving distribution of condoms, which by themselves are innocuous latex tubes used to prevent sexually transmitted diseases.

Looking Them in the Eye

Face-to-face interactions to win the support of decision makers and especially voters bring us into direct contact with people whose minds and votes we need to win to our cause. When we visit our elected representatives to ask for support, which is called lobbying, we can tell our stories and ask directly for his/her vote on an issue. When we interact with voters, either by knocking on doors in a voter canvass or distributing printed information like pamphlets and fliers in a high-traffic area like a grocery store or a mall, we can speak to neighbors directly about how a particular issue affects our lives. There is nothing—nothing—that is more potent than having direct eye contact with another human being, explaining ourselves, and then asking them to help us.

Media Matters

Mass media can be a powerful way to move messages to our base of supporters, nonaligned voters, and other decision makers. Through news and features articles, opinion pieces, paid advertising, editorials, and letters to the editor, we can augment and amplify our direct contacts with voters and lawmakers. But mass media also puts our information and compelling messages in front of our own base of supporters, who, whether actively engaged in the work or passively supportive or just plain unengaged, can be motivated to take action at an especially important time. Mass media exposure also gives visibility to the LGBT organizations that are carrying the workload, which in turn can lead to fruitful fund-raising opportunities.

Get Out the Vote

Electoral work increases the number of LGBT elected officials and rewards friends and punishes enemies, and elections remain a central element in our movement's strategy to achieve full equality under the law. With fewer than five hundred LGBT elected officials out of a total of five hundred thousand in the United States, we need more candidates to run for more offices. LGBT people hold less than .001 percent of all elected offices, and yet exit polling shows that we comprise up to 5 percent of the total electorate. Increasing the numbers of openly LGBT elected officials who will advocate on our behalf will inevitably change the outcomes on many legislative projects. LGBT organizers have learned much about political campaigns, both to elect our own candidates and to elect friends and throw enemies out of office. LGBT participation in the democratic processes of elections in the states of Massachusetts, California, New York, and Oregon has greatly strengthened legislative advocacy, because legislators respond to constituencies that help them stay in office, or conversely, fear constituencies that throw them out. Working in elections can be tedious, tiring, and unglamorous, but it's where the political rubber meets the road.

GAME PLAN FOR CHAPTER FOUR
LGBT Pride Events

Parades, marches, rallies, dances, cultural events, breakfasts and dinners, worship services, film festivals, community forums, and visibility actions are held in communities throughout the country under the broad category of "pride" events. Most of these events occur during the month of June and began as a way to remember and celebrate the Stonewall riots, a June 1969 three-night rebellion against New York City police raids on bars frequented by LGBT people. For example, the San Francisco Lesbian, Gay, Bisexual, Transgender Pride Celebration Committee declares its mission is "to educate the World, commemorate our heritage, celebrate our culture, and liberate our people." The San Francisco and New York City pride marches attract hundreds of thousands of participants every year. Since the first pride events in June 1970, these annual gatherings in virtually every major city and many medium-size and small cities have become must-attend events where the LGBT people of a city become visible to one another and to all other residents, and claim the strength and power of a community of lesbian, gay, bisexual, and transgender people. By typing "LGBT pride," or "gay pride" into your search engine, you can find many links to Web sites of organizing committees of major and minor pride events, including some events held on campuses of colleges and universities. You will also be able to link to the site of InterPride: the International Association of LGBT Pride Coordinators.

Try This at Home: Organize a Direct-Action Campaign

Imagine this scenario: A crisis has erupted on your campus. First, vandals struck against the Gay-Straight Alliance (GSA) by defacing the group's posters with sexually suggestive graffiti. Shortly after the vandalism, LGBT students reported a series of incidents of harassment, culminating in a loud and physical confrontation between two lesbian students and two straight male students on the quad. Pushing and shoving ensued that threatened to escalate into blows when passersby stepped in to break up the confrontation. The lesbian students later told campus police officers that the male students threatened them with sexual assault unless they stopped holding hands on campus. The male students also made derogatory sexual comments to the students who broke up the fight. Thus far, the campus police have refused to investigate the incident, despite the fact that the lesbian students gave the police complete descriptions and one of the passersby told the police that he heard the male students say they were going back to a particular dormitory, giving the police even more information. The administration has been silent on the issue, although other student groups, notably the campus women's organization and the African American student group, have spoken out about their members being harassed on campus, too.

In dealing with such a crisis, important steps can be taken in a direct-action campaign to address the specific incidents of harassment and violence against LGBT students and to build working alliances with other student organizations.

Call a meeting of the GSA and LGBT community. Invite all LGBT students and interested faculty and staff to come together. Students who are feeling most vulnerable will be upset and will no doubt express that. Set aside time at the beginning of the meeting so that those students can speak without interruption and without needing to explain their feelings or be challenged on facts. Invite a campus minister or someone from student health services to be on hand to offer students counseling or other help outside the meeting. Then, discuss both the most recent incidents of anti-LGBT vandalism and harassment, and any past incidents, to construct an accurate history and time line of the targeting of LGBT people on campus. Encourage attendees to share as much factual information as they have to build a common understanding of the scope of the problem and pay particular attention to the response from the campus police and the administration. Take notes so that an accurate record of the incidents can be used later. Brainstorm the concrete goals and action steps required to secure for LGBT people a safe learning, working, and living environment on campus. Formulate an action plan, putting completion of the steps on a schedule. Such steps should include:

- contacting the women's group and the African American student group, and other student organizations representing racial minorities on campus;

- utilizing the student newspaper to alert the campus community to safety concerns of women, African American, and LGBT students;
- holding a campuswide speak-out and rally against harassment, violence, and intimidation;
- circulating a petition during and after the speak-out/rally to build support for and put pressure on the administration to act swiftly and decisively on your demands;
- organizing a face-to-face meeting between administrators and the "campus safety" coalition to present specific demands ensuring the safety of all students;
- planning a follow-up component of the plan to monitor and assess the administration's response to your demands;
- setting a time/date/place for a follow-up meeting.

Build the coalition. Reach out to the campus women's group and the African American student group and any other student organizations that you know to be allies of LGBT people. All participating groups can then share information about forms of harassment that they have experienced on campus, with a recognition that harassment isn't limited to just one group of students. Any group that has put together an action plan should be encouraged to share it, so that plans are blended and adjusted to account for the needs, interests, and participation of all affected and supportive student groups. Have the coalition adopt a campaign name for its work, and have each organization appoint at least two representatives to the coalition. In this way, organizational representatives are empowered to speak on behalf of their home organizations and to commit resources of their organizations to the overall effort, subject to approval of their home group. The coalition should then be formally announced to the larger campus community.

Organize a campus-wide speak-out/rally. The speak-out gives an opportunity to those who have experienced harassment to be heard, and to declare zero-tolerance for harassment, intimidation, and violence. The speak-out/rally should be held in a noticeable public space on campus, preferably outdoors and near the location of at least one of the incidents. Make placards/signs expressing the central messages of your direct-action campaign: "Campus Safety for All" and "School Is No Place for Fear." In addition to personal testimony from targeted students, have organizational leaders from the coalition speak, making clear to the campus community and the administration that harassment and intimidation is a pressing issue for a number of students and student groups. Circulate petitions enumerating specific actions demanded of the administration.

Meet with the administration. The coalition should meet with campus administrators to present its demands, including that campus police take seriously the reported incidents of harassment and fully investigate all complaints, that the administration commit to sensitivity training for all campus security personnel, and that it commit its resources to make the campus safe for all. Some concrete actions that the administration can take include a poster campaign on campus that delivers a message of "respect for all," a program of student-led discussions in all dormitories about the school's zero tolerance for intimidation, harassment, and violence directed at students because of gender, race, sexual orientation, or gender variance, a commitment to fully investigate all reported incidents of harassment, and a commitment that disciplinary action will be taken against any students found to engage in harassment, intimidation, or violence against other students.

Evaluate the impact of the campaign. The coalition should assess how the campaign is affecting campus safety and consider what, if any, next steps are needed to hold the administration to its commitments. Remember that the typical pattern of student presence on campus for eight to nine months of the academic year can be to the benefit of an administration that does not want to take action, as does the natural transition in student leadership due to graduation. The campaign evaluation must include discussion of the next academic year and how leadership of the campaign can be transferred to students who will be on campus during the next fall term. Agree to have the coalition gather early at the start of the next academic year, sending a strong signal to the administration that its promises and commitments have not been forgotten.

Recognize gains by the administration. If the administration has taken positive steps and kept some or all of its commitments to deal with hostility in your campus environment, let them know that you appreciate the work and want to continue to build a strong working relationship with them.

Respond to the administration's failures. If the administration has avoided taking responsibility for the broader safety concerns on campus, there are still two important groups to mobilize on your behalf. First, the school's board of trustees has responsibility for setting broad policies for your school. While it may be unusual for student groups to present concerns about daily campus life to this group, the trustees can have an important role to play. Research the timing, location, and process of the trustee meetings to determine how best to approach this group. Second, most students on campus attend school with the support of their families. Your families have a natural interest in the safety of your campus. A few phone calls or letters from the families of students can powerfully capture an administrator's attention, especially if the calls and letters focus on the school's failure to create a safe environment for living and learning.

Resources for Campus Organizing

Organizing on college and university campuses has had a powerful influence on the political directions of the United States. Students participated in significant numbers in the black civil rights struggles of the 1950s and 1960s. Students organized in the 1960s and early 1970s to end the Vietnam War, a goal realized in 1975. Students led a campus-based divestment movement in the 1980s that resulted in many universities withdrawing investments in companies operating in apartheid-era South Africa. Never doubt that what you do on your campus can make a difference. Below are resources for the work.

LGBT Campus Organizing: A Comprehensive Manual, which was published in 1996, remains the definitive how-to manual for creating, stabilizing, and building the capacity of a student, faculty, staff, or alumni group on campus. The manual includes an organizing guide to domestic partnership, AIDS education, media, responding to homo-phobia, LGBT studies, and more, and can be downloaded at the Web site of the National Gay and Lesbian Task Force.

Campus Climate for Gay, Lesbian, Bisexual, and Transgender People: A National Perspective is a 2003 report by Susan R. Rankin that details the experiences of LGBT people at fourteen colleges and universities across the country. Based on a survey of nearly seventeen hundred students, faculty, and staff, *Campus Climate* documents experiences and perceptions of anti-LGBT bias and harassment, along with levels of institutional support for LGBT people. It highlights differences in experiences between various identity groups (e.g., students vs. faculty/staff, gays/lesbians vs. bisexuals, people of color vs. whites, etc.). Intended for administrators and others committed to creating an inclusive and supportive environment for LGBT people, *Campus Climate* concludes with a series of recommendations toward achieving this goal. It can be downloaded at the Web site of the National Gay and Lesbian Task Force.

Historically Black College and University Outreach Program, a project of the Human Rights Campaign Foundation, educates and organizes faculty, students, and staff at select historically black college and university (HBCU) campuses on gay, lesbian, bisexual, and transgender issues specific to each institution's needs. See the organization's Web site for more information.

Campus Pride is the only national nonprofit organization serving LGBT and ally student leaders at colleges and universities. Campus Pride started as an online community and resource clearinghouse under the name Campus PrideNet. In 2006 the organization broadened its outreach efforts and restructured as the current educational nonprofit organization Campus Pride. Type "Campus Pride" into your search engine to visit the Web site.

The United States Student Association (USSA) is the country's oldest and largest student organization. It hosts a number of caucuses, including the National Queer Student Coalition (NQSC). NQSC was created to ensure that the interests and voices of LGBT students are represented in USSA's governing body, and within the student movement on the national level. NQSC has organized in support of the Employment Non-Discrimination Act, the Hate Crimes Prevention Act, and in coalition with national LGBT associations. Type "United States Student Association" into your search engine to learn more.

Many national organizations have a special interest in campus organizing and provide resources to campus activists. Some of these are the Center for American Progress, People for the American Way, and the Feminist Majority Foundation, among many others. Pick an issue important to you and you are likely to find campus-related resources and information about it at your favorite organization's Web site.

5

Know Our Friends, Stand with Our Friends

Many gays, many lesbians, worked side by side with me in the civil rights movement. Am I supposed to tell them now thanks for risking their lives and their limbs to help me win my rights but that they are excluded because of the circumstances of their birth? Not a chance.

Julian Bond, president of the National Association
for the Advancement of Colored People, April 2, 2005

The LGBT political movement is blessed with good friends and allies, from individual women and men, to our parents, siblings, and family members, to faith leaders and communities, to organizations with memberships large and small. As organizers, our task is to continually nurture and grow the existing relationships and to seek support from new and untapped sources. When we ask for support from allies, we also offer support to them for the political projects that demand the bulk of their time and energy.

The LGBT community will never constitute a majority of people in this country, nor will we ever constitute a majority of voters. As a strategy for protecting and defending our equality under the law, expanding our bases of support is crucial to our success. But beyond the arithmetic of democracy, there is a compelling reason to reach out and ask non-LGBT people and organizations for help: Our Constitution promises that all Americans will be accorded equal protections of the law, equal access to the processes of democratic decision making, and equal opportunities for life, liberty, and happiness. The history of the

United States is littered with the failures to meet this promise and the disappointed and dejected people whose lives have been so tragically defined by those failures. It is in the interests of our country in living up to its promises to all that we join together to hold our leaders—and one another—accountable and to demand that the promises be kept. To make common cause with groups whose rights are violated and those people who have stood with them, we enter into working relationships with other communities' advocacy organizations. We, too, are called to account to make good on our pledge to support others' aspirations and dreams for full lives, free from prejudice and arbitrary discrimination. If we believe that LGBT people deserve lives not marred by prejudice and discrimination, then we respect and honor that others in society deserve the same.

People have organized to end injury and inequality on the basis of arbitrary and categorical distinctions such as sex, race, color, religion, national origin, language, physical abilities, mental capacities, income, age, and sexual orientation and gender expression since the founding of this country. Just as our nation's history reveals oppressions, our history also shows that people of all kinds join together to end them. The LGBT political movement joins this dignifying and uplifting history of resistance to oppression. We enter our own page into this history, but if we are doing our work as it should be done, we also are written into other communities' pages. Martin Luther King Jr. said, "The arc of history bends towards justice." But we who believe in justice hope to make it bend faster and further by working together.

Three fundamental principles govern our interactions with other organizations and communities that share similar goals for their people, the three R's of relationships among allies.

- *Respect.* We give to other communities the respect that we want given to ours. We listen before we speak. We learn before we pronounce. We open up to an expansive view of social change before we decide that an issue important to an ally does not deserve our attention.

• *Reciprocity.* We do with others what we want done with us. The surest way to forge enduring alliances is to show up, to support and help other organizations reach their goals.

• *Repetition.* We offer and give our help again and again. We ask for the help of others again and again. We show up again and again. We are consistent, constant, and continuous in our relationship-building work.

Building Durable Alliances: Our Toughest Task

No organizing task that faces us is more crucial to our success than building durable alliances with non-LGBT organizations, and especially those based in communities of color that also work toward an overarching goal of social justice. To fail to make strong working alliances with groups based in communities of color means that the LGBT movement will be isolated from important allies in the struggle for social justice and full equality, but also that our understanding of social justice will be shaped by mostly white and middle-class people. We develop and learn from a broadened and deepened vision of social justice when we join forces with those who have experienced a different kind of oppression. Finally, working with other oppressed groups on our issues *and* their issues brings us all closer to a society in which all people are treated with respect, dignity, and fairness. Although LGBT movement organizers and leaders have improved on the goal of alliance building, our movement historically has been only weakly and erratically committed to it, for several reasons.

First and most obvious, the LGBT movement has been primarily driven by middle-class and white LGBT people. Not only has this demographic reality caused a narrowing of our political vision, the dominance of white middle-class people has obscured the presence and leadership of LGBT people of color, leaving them relatively powerless to affect the development of our overall political agenda. While some LGBT colleagues of color have continued to participate in our movement, others have departed in frustration and disappointment. It is critically important, then, that white LGBT organizers listen carefully and attentively to LGBT organizers of color and learn from our colleagues of color what matters most in their organizing contexts. For example, the Audre Lorde Project, an organization by, for, and about LGBT people of color in New York City, is home to a program called TransJustice, which focuses on meeting the needs of transgender people of color. TransJustice organizes to support access to jobs, housing, and education for transgender people, transgender-sensitive healthcare, HIV-related services and job-training programs, and resists and responds to police, government, and anti-immigrant violence. Some white-dominated and lesbian- and gay-dominated groups might regard access to such basic needs as tangential to their agendas, but an organization dedicated to tending to its own communities of origin gives these basic needs high priority in their organizing program. Meeting the fundamental needs of people in a community is the fundamental reason for community organizing, whether the need is for a job or freedom from discrimination on the job.

Second, the decades-long internal debate within our movement regarding the definitions of what constitutes a legitimate "gay issue" has greatly impeded a movement-wide embrace of social issues that take us beyond the narrower confines of gay, only gay, and always gay. The "gay issues" debate ebbs and flows, but has remained a constant within our movement. The National Gay and Lesbian Task Force has frequently been criticized for expending its resources on so-called "nongay issues." For example, the organization's board of directors passed a resolution in 1991 opposing the Gulf War, undertaken by then president George H. W. Bush to repel an Iraqi invasion of Kuwait, a Persian Gulf oil producer and ally of the United States. The board members believed that the Gulf War was an international social justice issue demanding response from U.S. social justice organizations, that it would jeopardize LGB people in the armed forces, and that it would divert much-needed government resources away from domestic programs, including health care and AIDS research. The resolution was widely panned by a host of gay critics, who described it as a distraction from the organization's central mission of combating homophobia in the United States, and noted that the organization was the only LGBT national group to oppose the Gulf War. Some funders punished the organization with their checkbooks, withdrawing contributions from the Task Force.

A broader understanding of LGBT issues in social justice contexts has developed since 1991. In 1999, following the convictions of the two men accused of murdering gay Wyoming college student Matthew Shepard, the Task Force, and a dozen other LGBT organizations, took a strong stand against the death penalty, which had been sought by prosecutors in the Shepard case. Prosecutors had also sought the death penalty in the criminal sentencing of the men who murdered James Byrd Jr., a disabled African American man who died after being dragged behind a pickup truck in Jasper, Texas, in June 1998. There was little doubt that each crime was motivated by bias against gay people and African American people, respectively. In a February 1999 Task Force resolution against the imposition of the death penalty, both murders of Shepard and Byrd were described as hate crimes. The Task Force thirteen-point statement included these three key points: (1) the death penalty is disproportionately applied to poor people and people of color; (2) the death penalty does not improve a criminal-justice system that is plagued with inequities and discrimination against poor people, people of color, and other marginalized groups; and (3) the interests of the gay, lesbian, bisexual, and transgender community in protecting its members from acts of violence must not be construed as support for the death penalty. The Human Rights Campaign (HRC), which claims the largest membership and operating budget of any U.S. LGBT group, took no position. "We don't have a policy on the death penalty, and we don't see it as a particularly gay issue," Wayne Besson, then a spokesperson for HRC, told the *Boston Phoenix* in a story published on February 9, 2001.

In late 2002 as the administration of George W. Bush ramped up for war against Iraq, dozens of national and regional LGBT organizations took stands opposing the coming war, including the International Gay and Lesbian Human Rights Commission, the National Center for Lesbian Rights, the National Transgender Advocacy Coalition, the National Youth Advocacy Coalition, Pride at Work, the Al-Fatiha Foundation, and the National Gay and Lesbian Task Force. The Log Cabin Republicans, a group of gay and lesbian Republicans, lined up behind the Bush administration, supporting the "war on terror." The Human Rights Campaign proclaimed neutrality on the issue: "We believe such a statement [for or against war] would fall outside our specific mission, which is to ensure that gay, lesbian, bisexual, and transgendered people achieve equality in today's society" (*Advocate*, March 18, 2003).

LGBT organizations, in particular the National Gay and Lesbian Task Force, embrace other issues that cut along race and gender lines. In 1995 the Task Force threw its support behind affirmative action policies that call for extra efforts to be made to include people of color and women in applicant pools for jobs or admission to universities. The statement was issued the year before the nation's first state measure to ban all forms of affirmative action appeared on ballots in California in November 1996. The Task Force affirmed that "a healthy society, one in which homophobia can be eradicated, is a society which acknowledges and takes responsibility for its history of oppression and commits itself to eliminating discrimination for all people." In 2006, when immigration policies became the right wing's hot-button issue, the Task Force and other LGBT organizations spoke out strongly in support of immigrant-rights groups, noting that at least five hundred thousand of the estimated 12 million undocumented people in the United States are LGBT, and more than half of men and over one-third of women in same-sex couples in which both partners are Hispanic are not U.S. citizens. Immigration is indisputably an issue that affects LGBT people. The Task Force also called the right wing's deployment of immigration as a problem of crisis proportions a transparent effort to divert the country's attention away from the very real crises of a war in Iraq going very badly, soaring gasoline prices, and the failure to cope with the aftermath of the hurricane-related flooding of New Orleans.

This refusal by some LGBT organizations and organizers to step outside a narrow "gay" agenda to make connections around other human rights issues alienates friends and allies who work outside the LGBT context. When we fail to recognize and articulate a broader understanding of human rights as inseparable from our own interests, we do not join with others on a range of important issues that could bring us into direct contact and working relationships with social justice groups from other communities. When the Task Force and nine other LGBT organizations took the stand against the death penalty, we built common cause with the National Association for the Advancement of Colored People, the American Friends Service Committee, the American Civil Liberties Union, and a host of groups dedicated specifically to abolishing the death penalty in the United States. While LGBT groups will make distinct and separate decisions about when and how to align with other social justice movements and around what issues, a willingness to stand in solidarity with others is a fundamental requirement of building solid and lasting relationships outside our own movement.

Third, as organizers, we carry into this work our own prejudices, misperceptions, and assumptions about people with different physical abilities and people from other racial and ethnic communities, other class backgrounds, other genders, other cultures, and other language groups. We are human and our views of "others" are inescapably a part of how we view the world. But as organizers, we must continually examine our own prejudices, misperceptions, and assumptions and allow ourselves to challenge those prejudices by our own real and lived interactions with those not like ourselves. As LGBT organizers, we must rely on our confidence in the ability of people to change the way they think when we face changing the way we think.

We ask others to change how they think about us; we can change how we think about others. This kind of personal reflection and its attendant discomforts in revealing our prejudices can be a source of anxiety, guilt, and shame. And it simply must be done. We cannot create authentic and honest relationships with people different from ourselves if we can't stare into the mirror and see how our own presumptions about others limit us. This process, called prejudice reduction, can be engaged by reading about kinds of prejudices, participating in antiracism workshops, joining a reading group specifically dedicated to learning about other cultures, watching educational and popular films that accurately portray other cultures, and participating in community-based projects that work to bring people together across racial, class, and religious lines of difference. Irrespective of how we address our own prejudices, the single most important element that we bring to the task is a willingness to look within ourselves and to refrain from excusing or rationalizing or avoiding the internal accounting needed to move past prejudice.

No aspect of alliance building across racial, class, or religious lines comes easily, either to individuals or to social justice organizations. Within the LGBT community, the process is made even more difficult because our movement is dominated by white, middle-class people living relatively comfortable lives. The privileges of class and race shield those of us who are white and middle class from harsher realities of racism and economic inequality, allowing some of us to say that those issues are not our issues because those people are not our people. It takes a conscious effort and no small amount of determined commitment to listening to people not like us about what is important to them. Whether we build alliances through LGBT organizing or a different social justice movement, this is the nitty-gritty, unglamorous, but richly rewarding project to create a community and world in which we understand each other more fully, appreciate each other more deeply, and join together with greater conviction to end all manner of arbitrary discriminations and social injustices that continue to burden so many, including LGBT people.

What follows are four examples of both the rewards and the complexities of working in alliance with other social justice organizations. Such work is never easy, but it must be done.

The Japanese American Citizens League's Early Support for LGBT Issues

While examples of nongay organizational support for the LGBT movement abound, a most compelling story is that of the Japanese American

Citizens League (JACL) and its expanding support of LGBT people, issues, and communities. Founded in California in 1929 to end discrimination targeted specifically at persons of Japanese ancestry residing in the United States, the JACL faced a monumental task. In California, there were over one hundred statutes that limited the rights of anyone of Japanese ancestry. Organizations like the Grange Association and Sons of the Golden West exerted powerful influence on the state legislature and on Congress to limit participation and rights of Japanese Americans, largely to exclude them from competing for jobs in agriculture and other industries. The Japanese Exclusion League, founded in May 1905 under the name Asiatic Exclusion League, was established to rid California of its Japanese population, even those who were American citizens by birth.

But the JACL's greatest challenge came with the United States' entry into World War II, when the nation's anxieties about the outbreak of war with Japan found a vulnerable target in Americans of Japanese descent. Thousands were imprisoned in internment camps, suspected of disloyalty merely because of their ancestry. The JACL fought against the internments, but was no match for an aggressive and suspicious U.S. government that viewed Japanese Americans as dangerous aliens, no matter that many had become integral to cities and towns in which they lived. Japanese Americans also suffered under governmental hostility as expressed in laws forbidding marriages between persons of different races, laws not stricken down by the U.S. Supreme Court until 1965.

Nonetheless, the JACL fought on for its people. The organization joined the famed 1963 March on Washington led by Dr. Martin Luther King Jr. and other civil rights leaders. It advocated for the reform of marriage laws that finally came in the 1965 case *Loving v. Virginia.* In 1988 it won passage of federal legislation, called a redress bill, to give monetary compensation to Japanese Americans who had been incarcerated during World War II and to issue a formal governmental apology for this great injustice and humiliation.

With so much facing the JACL, we could perhaps accept and understand that taking LGBT-supportive positions just didn't make it onto their "to do" list. But the JACL did not avoid or shy away from the subject of LGBT rights, believing that social justice is meant for all. With little fanfare or notice from LGBT organizations, the JACL national board of directors in 1993 voted to endorse the right of openly gay and lesbian people to serve in the military. Early in 1994, the organization opposed over a dozen antigay ballot questions in cities and states in the Northwest. But also in 1994, the JACL became the first nongay civil rights organization in the United States to institute and affirm an organizational position that marriage is a fundamental human right that should be guaranteed to all. By failing to publicly acclaim these expressions of support from the JACL, we in the LGBT movement missed an important opportunity to leverage its support with other civil rights groups and to build a stronger bridge to Asian American communities more generally.

The LGBT organizations had not built a strong alliance with the JACL, but in the Congress, one openly gay member stood with them. Of special note in that organization's debates over same-sex marriage were the remarks of then congressman Norman Mineta, who would later serve in the cabinets of both Bill Clinton and George W. Bush. Mineta, himself interned in the World War II camps, praised the work of openly gay congressman Barney Frank to pass the 1988 bill making financial restitution and formal apology to formerly interned Japanese Americans: "Now here's a guy, openly gay member of Congress from Massachusetts, with only a very, very small Japanese American constituency. What did he do? He made redress his top priority. Why? Because he saw our civil rights as a fundamental principle. Doing what is right is often controversial, often unpopular. But if we are to remain a viable voice in the national civil rights movement, we cannot back away from our commitments simply because the issue is difficult" (quoted in *Nikkei Heritage*, summer 2002).

The lesson is clear. Mineta and members and leaders of the JACL affirmed the organization's position on same-sex marriage, in part because Barney Frank championed the redress bill. In politics, as in all other aspects of life, friends support friends and acts of courage and alliance with friends are noticed, appreciated, and reciprocated.

César Chávez: Labor Leader and Early Ally

Some charismatic leaders of allied movements take firm public stands that reverberate through their organizations and movements. César Chávez, the beloved founder and leader of the United Farm Workers (UFW), presents one such example. When he was a youngster, Chávez's family went from owning a prosperous farm in Arizona to becoming migrant crop pickers in California. Chávez completed only eighth grade before joining his parents in the fields. As an adult, Chávez worked for ten years for a migrant workers service organization and then founded the United Farm Workers in 1962, building from the ground up the first labor organization to better the lives of farm workers. Chávez expended his life force leading boycotts, workers' strikes, and voter registration and education drives, and tirelessly pursuing justice for his people. Beginning in the 1970s, Chávez joined with LGBT people. He spoke at the October 11, 1987, March on Washington for Lesbian and Gay Rights. On October 13, 1989, Chávez spoke at a Boston gathering to celebrate the founding of that city's LGBT labor organization, Gay and Lesbian Labor Activist Network (GALLAN). César Chávez died in 1993.

The legacy of his support for LGBT people and causes continues to inspire alliance-building between the UFW and LGBT groups. On June 16, 2005, Equality California, the state's LGBT political organization, announced support for a boycott of Gallo wines, which was led by the UFW to win fair treatment for grape pickers. Equality California showed up at the kickoff rally for the Gallo boycott. On June, 23, 2005, the United Farm Workers National Executive Board, in an unprecedented move, voted to endorse a California bill to make same-sex marriage legal in that state. César Chávez's granddaughter Christine Chávez, the UFW political director, spearheaded the drive to win the UFW endorsement. Christine Chávez stated, in a UFW press statement, "Beginning in the 1970s, before there was widespread public acceptance of gay people, especially among Latinos, my grandfather, César Chávez, spoke out strongly for gay rights. He attended gay rights rallies and marches. He brought with him the UFW's black-eagle flags and farm workers who wished to participate. There are certain lessons a granddaughter learned from growing up around her grandfather: You can't champion equality for your own people when you tolerate discrimination against any people because of who they are.... Freedom is indivisible."

Christine Chávez took a sabbatical from her post at the UFW to work with the state's LGBT political group, Equality California, during summer 2005, where she launched an organizing drive to build support for the same-sex marriage bill within Latino communities. Both the Senate and the Assembly ("House" in other states) of the California legislature later passed the bill, a historic first, and sent it to Governor Arnold Schwarzenegger's desk, where he delivered a deadly veto to the legislation. Christine Chávez, in July 2006, penned her name to a pro-same-sex-marriage advertising campaign entitled Marriage Matters.

The examples of the JACL and the Chávez legacy within the United Farm Workers told in this necessarily short form do not fully convey the considerable internal tensions and disagreements over pro-LGBT positions. Just as LGBT activists argue over what should be included in our political agenda, members of these groups, too, question whether LGBT issues are their issues. In the case of the JACL position on same-sex marriage, a proposal was made to retract the group's support for marriage equality. The retraction proposal was defeated, but only after long and heated debate that included statements like "this is not a Japanese American matter." Lia Shigemura, a former staff member of the JACL, countered in the November 2002 issue of Nikkei Heritage, "It's no wonder that many of you might believe that the issues of lesbians and gays are not real Japanese American issues, because many people like me, when we come out, are forced to leave organizations like the JACL."

Following the UFW announcement of its support for a bill to legalize same-sex marriage in California, rank-and-file farm workers criticized the union's move. One member of the union was quoted in the *Santa Cruz Sentinel* (June 29, 2005) as saying, "It just isn't right for a man to marry another man. The only law that should be followed is the law from God." In the same article, Christine Chávez responded to the criticism. "It's that plain and simple," she said. "We are a civil rights organization, and we need to take a stance and take leadership. We shouldn't deny people marriage if they've been in a committed relationship and they want to get married."

African Americans and LGBT Rights

Many titans of the African American civil rights movement stand solidly with LGBT people on a range of equality issues. These leaders who speak forthrightly in support of LGBT people and rights include Julian Bond, the chair of the NAACP, Democratic congressman John Lewis of Georgia, a former leader of the famed Student Non-Violent Coordinating Committee, Rev. Joseph Lowery of the Southern Christian Leadership Conference, and the late Coretta Scott King, widow of Dr. Martin Luther King Jr. This list includes other black church leaders, academics and writers, elected officials, Hollywood personalities like Whoopi Goldberg, and former officials of presidential administrations like Joycelyn Elders, who served as surgeon general of the United States under President Clinton. The Congressional Black Caucus, a powerful group of African American legislators within the U.S. Congress, has consistently supported LGBT legislative efforts. But the African American community leadership is not unified around support for LGBT issues, especially same-sex marriage. As important as the LGBT-supportive positions of these leaders are, they do not fully reflect the profound differences of opinion among black Americans about homosexuality and its meaning in society.

African Americans' ambivalent response to comparisons of the social positions of black people and LGBT people and a generalized dis-

comfort among many black Americans about homosexuality is illus-
trated in positions taken by the NAACP. The NAACP's lobbyists have
urged passage of the federal bill to ban discrimination against LGBT
people in employment. The NAACP testified strongly against the Federal Marriage Amendment at a Senate subcommittee hearing on March
3, 2004. But the nation's foremost organization by, for, and about black
Americans has yet to take up the issue of same-sex marriage at its annual convention, despite an ever-growing list of community leaders,
including its own president, Julian Bond, who support the right of
same-sex couples to marry. By contrast, the California chapter of the
NAACP voted at its state convention in October 2004 to endorse the
right to marry for same-sex couples, becoming the first local or state
NAACP chapter to do so. The social approval of same-sex relationships
gained through legal marriage acts as a dividing, not a uniting, issue for
black Americans.

Social scientists show that African American support for LGBT
rights to work, to secure housing, and to have equal access to public accommodations remains strong, while a majority views homosexuality
as wrong. Researcher G. B. Lewis, in a 2003 study titled "Black-White
Differences in Attitudes toward Homosexuality and Gay Rights," published in *Public Opinion Quarterly*, wrote, "Blacks appear to be more
likely than Whites to both see homosexuality as wrong and to favor gay
rights." Lewis speculated that a deep opposition to discrimination in
political and economic spheres accounts for the strong support for
nondiscrimination measures. A follow-up to Lewis's study by Charles
Negy, published in the *Journal of Sex Research* in November 2005, found
that the more they attended church, the more negative were the attitudes of African Americans to homosexuality.

Polling information released by the Pew Research Center on August
3, 2006, shows that, among African Americans who identify as Protestants, 74 percent oppose gay marriage; civil unions, a status that confers
all/most legal rights of marriage, is opposed by 62 percent of the black
Protestants who were polled. These figures of African American opposition to both same-sex marriage and civil unions can be contrasted

with the 56 percent of respondents of all races who oppose same-sex marriage and 42 percent of respondents of all races who oppose civil unions. The Pew poll did not include questions about other forms of nondiscrimination goals of LGBT people. But the poll results and the social science data suggest a relationship between churchgoing and disapproval of homosexuality, despite recognitions that LGBT people deserve to be treated fairly.

The divide in black support for straightforward equality claims like fair employment and black opposition to same-sex marriage can be seen as one consequence of an ongoing hostile social climate for black families. When black families, especially black families headed by women, are blamed for a host of social ills, including urban crime, drug use, and teenage pregnancy rates, it is no wonder that some African American leaders would respond by closing ranks around their ideal of family as a married couple with children. Any deviation from or doubts about that traditional model of ideal family could be seen as an attack on the community leaders' efforts to shore up that model within their own communities.

The central role in African American communities of black churches and their pastors gives religious weight and context to the defense and promotion of traditional family structures. Some black pastors have been harsh in their rhetoric, identifying homosexuality as an attack on black families and black community. Rev. Willie Wilson, a pastor at Union Temple Baptist Church in Washington, D.C., delivered a July 2005 sermon at his church in which he blamed lesbians and income-earning women for problems in the black community. Preached Wilson, as quoted in the *Washington Blade*, July 15, 2005, "We live in a time when our brothers have been so put down, can't get a job, lot of the sisters making more money than brothers. And it's creating problems in families. That's one of the reasons our families breaking up. And that's one of the reasons many of our women are becoming lesbians. You got to be careful when you say you don't need no man. I can make it by myself. Well, if you don't need a man, what's left? Lesbianism is about to take over our community." LGBT African American leaders and commentators sharply rebuked Wilson, but he was unrepentant. In a statement published in the *Washington Post* on July 30, 2005, elaborating on his outrageous claims, Wilson wrote, "I am not homophobic, nor am I an antifeminist; rather I am deeply concerned about the future of our children and the future of the Black family."

While not all African American promoters of black traditional families express such unforgiving condemnations of homosexuality, other more moderate black leaders look askance at LGBT advocacy for the right to marry, even while they have supported other LGBT rights concerns. The Reverend Jesse Jackson, for instance, supports most of our equality claims, but takes exception to legal marriage for same-sex couples. Jackson ran for president in 1984 and embraced and welcomed LGBT people to his campaign, as staff, donors, and supporters. During that race, Jackson was unequivocal in his language and speech that he stood shoulder-to-shoulder with LGBT people, saying repeatedly and in many contexts that we were part of his Rainbow Coalition. But Jackson, in February 2004, spoke out against same-sex marriage. During an appearance at Harvard Law School in Cambridge, Massachusetts, Jackson said, as quoted in the *Boston Globe*, February 17, 2004, "The comparison with slavery is a stretch in that some slave masters were gay, in that gays were never called three-fifths human in the Constitution . . . and in that they did not require the Voting Rights Act to have the rights to vote. What is the same is that we all as citizens have the right to choose our partners."

Other black leaders unequivocally express their support. Massachusetts state senator Dianne Wilkerson gave an impassioned speech on February 12, 2004, during the Constitutional Convention debate over an amendment to outlaw same-sex marriage. She spoke of growing up black in Arkansas and shared with her colleagues in the legislature that her mother was not allowed to give birth in a public hospital due to strict segregation laws in place at the time. As reported by the *Boston Globe* on February 12, 2004, Wilkerson said, "I know the pain of being less than equal and I can not and will not impose that status on anyone else. I was but one generation removed from an existence in slavery. I could not in good conscience ever vote to send anyone to that place from which my family fled."

The confusing and contradictory views of homosexuality and LGBT equality claims have emerged within the family of Dr. Martin Luther King Jr. King himself made no recorded statements about LGBT people or LGBT communities. King's career as a civil rights leader, before his assassination in 1968, predates the rise of the LGBT political movement following the Stonewall riots in 1969. But King's close associate Bayard Rustin was a gay man whom King entrusted with many significant projects, including organizing the 1963 March on Washington, even while other civil rights leaders regarded Rustin as a pariah due to a conviction on a sex-related charge in the early 1950s.

King's widow, Coretta Scott King, was outspoken in her support for LGBT people, saying on numerous occasions that her late husband would, had he lived long enough, have stood with the LGBT communities. As reported by Reuters on March 31, 1998, Mrs. King said, "I still hear people say that I should not be talking about the rights of lesbian and gay people and I should stick to the issue of racial justice. But I hasten to remind them that Martin Luther King Jr. said, 'Injustice anywhere is a threat to justice everywhere.' I appeal to everyone who believes in Martin Luther King Jr.'s dream to make room at the table of brother- and sisterhood for lesbian and gay people."

Coretta Scott King died in 2006. Her daughter Bernice King persuaded her siblings that Mrs. King's funeral be held at New Birth Missionary Baptist Church in Lithonia, Georgia. Dr. King's funeral, and those of his parents, had taken place at the family's ancestral church home of Ebenezer Baptist Church in Atlanta. New Birth, a megachurch of twenty-five thousand members, is led by Bishop Eddie Long, a fundamentalist minister who had organized and led a demonstration opposing same-sex marriage in late 2004. Bernice King is an elder at New Birth and participated in the 2004 march against gay marriage, leading off the procession that began at Martin Luther King Jr.'s gravesite in Atlanta. Julian Bond, the president of the NAACP, declined to attend the funeral of his friend Mrs. King because it was held in the church of an antigay minister.

LGBT advocates struggle against the "almost but not quite" perspective of some black leaders regarding the aspirations of LGBT people, as evidenced in Rev. Jesse Jackson's statement on same-sex marriage. We are almost but not quite deserving of full legal equality, especially as regards marriage, because in our own history of prejudice and discrimination, we did not suffer the same subjugations as black Americans. The most effective responses to "almost but not quite" arguments to deny fundamental rights to LGBT people come from African American LGBT people. While allies like Senator Wilkerson can speak from their own experiences of racial discrimination, the words of black LGBT people who claim their rightful places in their communities of origin reverberate in a very different way.

Keith Boykin, an African American writer and gay leader who served in the Clinton administration, wrote, "The issues that affect Black gays and lesbians are issues that affect all Black people. Last year I sat in the living room of a young mother who had lost her child to violence in Newark, New Jersey. Her fifteen-year-old daughter, Sakia Gunn, was murdered because the killer thought she was gay. When black homosexuals and bisexuals are murdered, black heterosexual family members still have to bury their kin. . . . When Black people were forced to sit in the back of the bus, Black gay people were forced to sit in the back of the bus. When Black people could not vote, Black lesbians could not vote. And when Black people are beaten and abused by the police, Black bisexuals are beaten and abused by the police." (See "The Speech That Didn't Happen," remarks for the Millions More Movement March, October 15, 2005, on Boykin's Web site.)

Dialogues within the African American community will challenge and change the ambivalence that defines that community's stance toward LGBT people. As Julian Bond observed, "I think the black community is going to become more accepting, more tolerant. I can't place a timetable on it, but I'll tell you one thing: It depends on the degree to which black gays and lesbians begin to stand up in their churches, in their organizations, and say, 'This is me you're talking about.' That's a powerful, powerful message" (*Village Voice*, May 24, 2004).

In June 2006, the National Black Justice Coalition (NBJC), a nationwide advocacy organization by, for, and about African American LGBT people, launched a project to encourage black churches, the center of black community life in many cities and towns, to include openly LGBT people in their congregations and ministries. The organization also formed a Religious Advisory Committee to challenge anti-LGBT rhetoric in religious contexts. "The pulpit should be a place of love and not hate," said H. Alexander Robinson, NBJC's executive director, in a press release in June 2006. "Black communities face significant challenges from outside and within our communities. To face these challenges it is essential that Black churches be sanctuaries for the downtrodden and oppressed and vehicles for our emancipation."

While the intracommunity organizing led by African Amercian LGBT people proceeds, we can continue to build working alliances around the issues already supported broadly by black Americans and of great concern for our movement: fair employment practices, an end to bias violence, access to jobs and job training, full funding for AIDS/HIV programs, access to decent affordable housing, and a health care system that delivers for all.

The ACLU: Our First and Strongest Friend

In the pantheon of allies of LGBT people, the American Civil Liberties Union has no equal. The ACLU, a nongovernmental organization devoted to defending civil liberties in the United States, has been with us for longer than any other organization. The ACLU developed a full LGBT civil rights docket in 1956 and launched its LGBT and AIDS Project in 1986. The ACLU has been involved in nearly every conceivable issue relating to LGBT lives, and often on its own. Its entry into LGBT issues began with a recognition that the civil liberties guaranteed under the Bill of Rights were routinely denied LGBT people. In the 1950s, police and other public authorities violated LGBT peoples' rights to express their sexuality and to assemble in bars and clubs. The ACLU challenged sodomy laws and laws making public cross-dressing illegal. The organization worked to end discriminatory immigration laws that sometimes resulted in deportations of openly gay people. More recently, ACLU state chapters have worked for passage of nondiscrimination laws and the establishment of programs to make schools safe for LGBT students. In both the courts and the legislatures, the ACLU is usually on our side.

With striking ethical clarity and unwavering consistency, the ACLU protects civil liberties without regard to the popularity of those whose rights are being defended. In the incipient stirrings of LGBT movement and consciousness, there was no better friend than the ACLU; for decades, the ACLU was our only friend. But the organization's unwavering defense of the civil liberties of all people in this country takes it in some unexpected and not always well-understood directions. For example, the ACLU has repeatedly refused to endorse proposed laws to punish crimes motivated by hate, if prosecutors could use evidence of hate speech or association with hate groups to bring their cases to court, on the grounds that speech and free association are fundamental liberties. It opposes campus codes of speech that seek to discourage hate speech, including anti-LGBT speech and expression. The ACLU also opposes recently enacted laws that forbid demonstrations at funerals, such as those led by Rev. Fred Phelps and his clan, who demonstrate at the funerals of LGBT people and servicemembers killed in Iraq. The ACLU has defended the right of Nazis to march through largely Jewish neighborhoods, much to the dismay of some Jewish leaders. The ACLU adheres to its mission of defending the rights of speech, expression, and assembly even when the people it defends engage in the kinds of expressions that LGBT people regard as defamatory and hurtful. In its view, divisive expressions of hate and bigotry are best countered by expressions of tolerance, equality, and fairness, rather than infringing on anyone's right to speak.

The ACLU remains a strong ally, even while the organization takes an occasional position that seemingly conflicts with a stated goal of the LGBT movement. In 1985, the ACLU National Board of Directors passed the following policy, as posted on its Web site: "The ACLU supports legal recognition of lesbian and gay relationships, including the right to marry. Such recognition is imperative for the complete legal equality of lesbian and gay individuals." It was the first national advocacy organization, LGBT or nongay, to do so.

Founded in 1920, the ACLU has an affiliate chapter in each state and Puerto Rico, plus chapters on college and university campuses around the country. In states where the LGBT movement remains relatively weak, the ACLU affiliate often serves as a consolidating resource for LGBT activists and organizers.

Lessons Learned, Moving Forward

The history of LGBT organizations' relationships with allies show both successes and failures, weaknesses and strengths. When engaging in organizing work, it is crucial to honestly assess our work, learn from it, and move forward. Had our LGBT organizations reached out to potential allies and collaborated with them to help them achieve some of their goals, we might now be in a stronger position to call on them for help in contemporary battles, especially in the state-level ballot-initiative campaigns that have resulted in a discouraging string of losses. Some movement leaders recognize that our failure to do this alliance-building work decades ago comes back to haunt us today. Matt Foreman of the National Gay and Lesbian Task Force put it this way in a Task Force newsletter of summer 2006: "Starting in the 1970s, we all could have done a much better job in working for racial and economic justice so that when the attacks came, we would have had an army of allies defending us. We ... could have recognized that the only way to win and hold power is to strengthen the grassroots and invest heavily in state and local organizing."

When the Japanese American Citizens League passed the redress bill, it had the support and help of openly gay congressman Barney Frank, but no LGBT political organization joined that fight. In 1988, our national groups were tiny and desperately underfunded, especially in comparison with the staffs and budgets they wield today. Our federal legislative agenda, the arena in which the JACL worked to pass the redress bill, focused on two main issues: funding to support AIDS research and AIDS service programs, and passage of the 1989 Hate Crimes Statistics Act. Most of the LGBT federal legislative work was managed by a small handful of staffers at the National Gay and Lesbian Task Force and the then Human Rights Campaign Fund. In 1988, very few state-level LGBT organizations existed at all, so almost no base of support in the states could be mobilized. Had JACL asked for help from the LGBT organizations in 1988, there would have been little to offer. Fortunately, our LGBT organizations have grown and proliferated at national, state, and local levels, and we now have more to offer when allies ask us for help. We have learned these hard lessons about working with allies and we are moving forward. Below are guidelines for making and keeping friends.

Seek out ways to help allied organizations. Pay attention to the work that our allies see as priorities for their communities. Through the media, through participation in social justice coalitions, through our personal contacts, seek out ways to support the causes others care most about. Educate yourself and your organization's members about the concerns of allied groups. Attend forums and community informational events hosted by your allied organizations to learn about them and from them.

Make the offer of help before being asked. Offering a friendly organization help with a project builds greater friendship. Organizers love nothing so much as an unsolicited offer of help. Reach out to other social justice organizations in your community or on your campus. To do so shows that we understand how their social justice goals harmonize with our own and we break the isolation that organizers so often experience in doing their work. Offer your group's endorsement, mobilize your members to show up for allies' events, sign on to support statements, write letters to newspapers about your allies' issues, speak out about social justice.

Show up! Make the effort to show up for important events on the calendars of allied groups. LGBT organizations of every size can establish working groups or committees charged with mobilizing members to show up at demonstrations, rallies, and meetings called by our allies. Committing our own time and effort means much.

Understand and appreciate the capacity of allies. What is asked of allied organizations needs to be within the range of the groups' capacities to deliver help. It does none of us any good to ask for help that is beyond an organization's resources, time, and energy. For example, asking allies to sign a petition may be a better request than asking allies to circulate the petition among their own memberships. Engage leaders of allied groups in discussions about what they can do to help, rather than assuming their help can only come in the way that we would most want. No offer of help is too small to accept. We may ask for small kinds of support from small organizations, but their ability to give can grow as the organization grows.

Ask for help on issues of agreement and common cause. No allied organization will help us if they don't agree with us on an issue. Go to allies or potential allies with an issue they already support. Churches in minority communities may want to join campaigns about AIDS prevention or bias crime reduction or violence prevention. Start with what interests a potential ally and build the relationship from that point of agreement. Starting with a common cause creates trust and friendship that sometimes opens a door to discussing other issues.

Accept that some disappointments will happen, but resist disillusionment. We're working with people, after all, so we will be disappointed if an ally breaks a commitment or can't turn out members for an event. When we are disappointed, it is important to check back and to find out what happened and how we can make sure it doesn't happen again.

Checking in with our allies shows we care about them and that we need their help. Disappointments, though, can't be allowed to turn to disillusionment about the value of allies. We need them; they need us. We all need to find the best ways of working together.

Value and recognize what our friends do for us. When members of an allied organization join us in an important struggle, recognize them, thank them, and include them in future projects. If a press release will be issued announcing an important development in an ongoing struggle, be sure to name all the groups that worked in concert. Be specific about what the allied organizations have contributed and, if possible, include a quote from the leaders of your closest allied organizations. Having a party to celebrate a big victory? Invite your allies to party with you. Holding a rally to build broad support for your goal? Invite leaders of allied groups to speak at the rally. Thank allies in every way we would want to be thanked. Keep friends updated on progress and ask them for help again.

Ask for feedback, advice, and organizing tips. Our allied organizations are home to organizers. Ask them how they would manage a difficult issue or what their experience with a particularly stubborn opponent has been or how they achieved their greatest success. Turn to them for advice. Find out how they assess your organizing work. Invite them to review materials, plans, and strategies. If appropriate, invite them to participate in making decisions at key moments in your campaign. Organizing is more an art than a science, more a process than a product. Let others teach us.

Keep faithful to a broad vision of social justice. Pledging our allegiance to a broad vision of social justice that includes the goals and aspirations of all disadvantaged communities will keep us true to our work of building alliances. An ever more narrow view of what constitutes legitimate "gay" issues hampers our ability to make and keep good friends in other social justice movements. As has been articulated so eloquently by others, justice is indivisible. We champion equality and freedom for ourselves and others.

GAME PLAN FOR CHAPTER FIVE
Unlearning Our Prejudices

To engage with peers and colleagues across lines of race, class, gender, and physical ability often requires that organizers and activists do some self-reflection about the prejudices that we've learned. This process has different names: unlearning racism, antiprejudice education, prejudice reduction, anti-oppression, challenging white supremacy, antisexism, class analysis, diversity and disability education, and antiracism. All these philosophies share the perspective that taking a closer look at our own prejudices makes us more aware of how these prejudices can keep us from developing honest and strong working relationships with people not like ourselves. In a movement that seeks equality and justice, working across social boundaries that have divided us is imperative to building a powerful and unified social justice movement.

In many cities and on many campuses, organizations with a special mission to reduce bias, prejudice, and bigotry offer training, workshops, and materials that help in both the personal processes and the institutional processes of change. By typing any of the key words in the paragraph above into your search engine, you can find local and national organizations and resources about prejudice reduction. Some of these groups are the Student Environmental Action Coalition, Magenta Foundation's Crosspoint Anti Racism, School of the Americas Watch, Stop the Hate, National Conference on Community and Justice, and the Southern Poverty Law Center's Tolerance.org. The Tolerance.org project of the Southern Poverty Law Center maintains a particularly large and varied resource listing, inclusive of both community and campus-based action ideas that address a broad range of prejudices and bias, from racism to anti-Semitism to homophobia to ableism, in community settings both large and small.

Try This at Home: Start a Social Justice/Action Study Group

Organize a group of friends and colleagues both to discuss current social justice issues and also to expand your own understandings and knowledge base about our many allied movements. The group can serve as a resource to its members and a sounding board where opportunities for strategic alliances can be considered and thought through together. Let's get started.

Talk to people you know who share your interest in social justice and social change. You might start with other members of your home organization, whether it is community-based or campus-based. Or, if you belong to a faith community, reach out to the people with whom you worship.

Form a group. Invite eight to ten people to get together to talk about how a social justice study group can help you better understand the current political environment, issues that are hot topics in your community or in the country, and how a social justice perspective can guide both personal opinions and organizational decisions.

Decide on discussion parameters. At the first gathering, determine how frequently you will meet and what criteria will guide your choices or reading material that will help to frame your discussions. The group might choose to focus on the history of social justice organizing in the United States, and even more specifically, study in some depth one particular movement. Or the group could prioritize the current political landscape, choosing to read about contemporary issues that appear in news outlets every day. Or the group could choose to examine racial dynamics in society. But no matter how the group focuses itself, each member can take responsibility for identifying the readings for one meeting and leading that meeting's discussion.

Foster participation. Set the time/dates for as many meetings as there are group members. In this way, the group agrees to meet for as many times as required for each person to choose reading material and lead a discussion. Agree that at the end of that time frame, the group will spend at least one meeting reflecting on the value of the study group to each member's work and thinking and whether to continue into a second round of reading and discussion.

Make connections. Allow two hours for each meeting so that there is space and time to review the reading and highlight its most important points, discuss the meaning of the reading as it relates to the activities and agenda and dynamics within your organization or congregation, and consider whether and how the reading informs organizational goals. For example, if the study group has chosen to focus on the issue of immigration policies, the readings and discussions might shed light on how an organization could support the movement for fair and equitable treatment of immigrants. Or if the study group focuses on the history of the movement for women's rights and equality, it might be fruitful to talk through the connections between the goals of the women's movement and the LGBT movement, especially reproductive choice and control of one's own body. If the group has focused on an examination of racism and racial dynamics, members may feel it is time to bring these issues forward in the larger context of LGBT organizing in the community. Let both the readings and the discussion stimulate reflections about what is happening right now in an organization, a community, and the larger social and political environments of the country.

6

God Is a Weapon

LGBT organizers face an array of opposition organizations that claim millions of supporters, have access to astonishing resources, and have successfully insinuated LGBT issues into an overarching right-wing political agenda. Our adversaries on the right have become a powerful tail wagging the dog of mainstream politics through their persistent and dedicated work to elect politicians willing to support anti-LGBT legislative and policy initiatives. Most fearsome has been the rise of a powerful religiously based movement that is unrelenting in its pursuit of the disappearance of homosexuality and gender variance in society. The Christian right-wing anti-LGBT movement deploys God as a weapon against us.

Matt Foreman, the executive director of the National Gay and Lesbian Task Force, calls this massing of anti-LGBT resources and energy the "Antigay Industry," a formidable foe that can intimidate even the hardiest LGBT activists. By "industry," Foreman refers to the network of anti-LGBT organizations that produce and distribute materials and messages intended to stop progress on LGBT issues and to drive us back into silence and invisibility. Utilizing media outlets like radio, television, and print, the Antigay Industry churns out a standardized condemnation of homosexuality, mobilizing their listeners and readers to act against us in political spheres.

We can better understand the contemporary Antigay Industry by looking into its past. While most U.S. Christian churches and ministers have historically condemned homosexuality and all sex outside of marriage, beginning in 1978 with Anita Bryant's Save Our Children campaigns, a new kind of Christianized political campaign against us took shape. Bryant wanted to repeal a countywide nondiscrimination ordinance that had been passed in 1977 in Dade County, Florida, where she lived. In many cities and states, citizens can place on the ballot proposals to repeal or to pass laws, allowing all the voters of a jurisdiction to cast yes or no votes. Rallying other opponents of the law through church-based organizing and outreach, Bryant put the new nondiscrimination law up to popular vote in Dade County and she won, repealing the law. From this victory, she exported her special brand of Christianized anti-gay politics to a handful of other cities, repealing local nondiscrimination laws in three more cities. Bryant's right-wing anti-LGBT campaign was joined by California state senator John Briggs, whose 1978 proposal to ban lesbian and gay teachers from public schools was defeated by voters in that state. Since Bryant's innovative fusing of Christian fundamentalist theology with political campaigns, our efforts to win equality have been challenged repeatedly by an increasingly Christianized anti-LGBT movement in the courts, in legislatures, at the ballot box, and in public debate and discourse.

This dangerous mixing of God and politics accelerated in the 1980s, when the AIDS epidemic provided our adversaries with a pressing public health crisis to rationalize their call for the incarceration of gay men as a way to control the spread of the epidemic. A 1986 publication by Summit Ministries called *Special Report: AIDS*, concluded, "We might well prepare holding camps for all sexually active homosexuals with special camps for homosexuals with AIDS." AIDS and public health advocates successfully opposed this and other wildly draconian proposals to control the epidemic, including tattooing the buttocks of sexually active gay men.

In the late 1980s, right-wing organizers revived Bryant's tactic of putting the rights of LGBT people up for popular vote. Since the early 1990s, they have placed over one hundred ballot questions on various LGBT issues before voters, at the municipal, county, and state levels, winning nearly all of these ballot-question campaigns, typically by overwhelming majorities of votes. The anti-LGBT movement's successful use of ballot-question campaigns has drained community resources, exhausted organizers, damaged LGBT community-based organizations, and skewered us through countless public defamations of our lives and our dignity. But LGBT organizers have also learned much on the ballot-question campaign trails and have scored a dozen victories in campaigns concerning nondiscrimination laws since 2002.

The Christian right-wing anti-LGBT groups have become a major force in American politics. Focus on the Family, the Christian Coalition, the Traditional Values Coalition, the American Family Association, Concerned Women for America, American Vision, and a plethora of smaller national, state, and local organizations promote the idea that homosexuality and a healthful American society cannot coexist. Their entry into mainstream politics since the 1970s has been breathtaking. Under the leadership of James Dobson (Focus on the Family founder), Pat Robertson (Christian Coalition founder), Jerry Falwell (founder of the now-defunct Moral Majority), Lou Sheldon of Traditional Values Coalition, and Donald Wildmon (American Family Association founder), the Christianized right-wing anti-LGBT coalition commands the attention of the Republican Party at the very highest levels and, consequently, the national news media. These anti-LGBT leaders and their lieutenants train and mobilize local organizers, launch boycotts against LGBT-friendly companies, lobby legislators to oppose pro-LGBT bills, and inspire their followers to support candidates who share their view that homosexuality must be vilified and punished. At every turn, they oppose us, no matter the specific issue, no matter how reasonable our goals.

A Defining Struggle

The contemporary escalation of the Christian right-wing anti-LGBT movement followed closely the July 2003 U.S. Supreme Court decision in *Lawrence v. Texas* that struck down sodomy laws and the November 2003 Massachusetts Supreme Judicial Court decision in *Goodridge v. Department of Public Health* that declared unconstitutional marriage laws barring same-sex couples from obtaining marriage licenses. In particular, Focus on the Family, the Colorado Springs organization led by James Dobson, greatly increased its political capacity with the formation of the Focus on the Family Action Fund, enabling it to make monetary contributions and engage in direct political activity on behalf of candidates, including President George W. Bush during his 2004 reelection campaign.

For our adversaries, these two court decisions, seen as twin threats to a fundamentalist Christian vision of correct living, drew a stark and bright line of struggle. Lou Sheldon, founder and leader of the right-wing Traditional Values Coalition, said, "America stands at a defining moment. The only comparison is our battle for independence" (quoted in Bob Moser, "Holy War," *Southern Poverty Law Center Intelligence Report*, spring 2005). Other right-wing leaders echoed Sheldon's fierce call to defend and protect the exclusively heterosexual institution of marriage, resulting in the 2003 introduction of the Federal Marriage Amendment and the 2004 general election results of eleven states passing constitutional amendments to ban same-sex marriage. The Federal Marriage Amendment has been defeated twice in the U.S. Congress, but stands as a unifying organizing project of the Antigay Industry and a rallying point around which conservative anti-LGBT organizers can mobilize their base of support in election season.

Resource Mismatch and a Cultural Hangover

In an August 2004 follow-up report on the major Christian right-wing organizations, the National Gay and Lesbian Task Force compared the financial resources of thirteen sponsoring organizations with those of thirteen leading national LGBT organizations. The report, titled *Marriage Protection Week Sponsors*, showed that the largest anti-LGBT organizations had a combined income of $217 million, as compared to $54 million combined income of the thirteen LGBT groups. The budgets of LGBT advocacy groups are dwarfed by those of our adversaries. In part, this vast difference in resources stems from the ability of our religiously based adversaries to communicate regularly with their mem-

bers, sometimes on a daily basis, giving them ready access to supporters who will donate money to the cause. The electronic media networks
owned and operated by anti-LGBT groups, especially radio, provide a
steady stream of programs that guide and shape their listeners' views
of homosexuality and other social issues and offer folksy advice about
child-rearing and other family concerns. In significant ways, Christian
fundamentalist preachers and organizations become an indispensable
source of guidance and companionship, nurturing a fierce loyalty even
among people whose only contact is through media. By contrast, LGBT
organizations communicate primarily through written materials, either in print or on the Internet, both much less immediate and personal
forms of contact. The communication advantage of the Christian right-
wing groups translates into much greater monetary rewards from their
base. The Christian anti-LGBT movement enjoys yet another structural
advantage over our movement: it builds upon a profound shared sense
of purpose cultivated through weekly church attendance in congregations led by a pastor known, trusted, and financially supported by
the congregants. The access and seemingly unassailable authority of
grassroots Christian right-wing leaders to their followers remains un-
matched by that of LGBT community leaders.

But our adversaries don't only rely on having more money to spend.
They have more people too. Analysis by CNN of voter turnout in the
2004 general election, during which Bush won reelection and eleven
states passed constitutional amendments banning same-sex marriage,
reveals that white evangelical voters made up 23 percent of the electorate
and gave Bush 36 percent of his votes. By comparison, 4 percent of 2004
voters identified as lesbian, gay, or bisexual. (Transgender was not an
offered choice.) LGB voters gave about 75 percent of their votes to John
Kerry, constituting about 6 percent of his votes. These numbers alone
do not present a comprehensive picture of overall support for LGBT issues. Polls identifying only LGB voters leave out non-LGB voters who
support LGBT issues. Similarly, the figures for combined budgets of the
anti-LGBT organizations and LGBT organizations does not account
for the budgets of non-LGBT groups that are staunch allies of LGBT

groups. Nonetheless, the figures illustrate that, when it comes to the money and people that translate into political power, we operate at a significant resource deficit.

Beyond the resource discrepancy, LGBT organizers and allies also grapple with the cultural hangover from centuries of social opprobrium and animus directed at LGBT people. While we celebrate victories large and small, the cultural shadow cast over us remains deep and it will not be dispelled through a series of legal and political victories. Our adversaries come to every skirmish with generations of social disapproval of homosexuality backing up their condemnations of homosexuality. Viewed in this light, the mostly lopsided popular-vote counts, when an aspect of our civil rights reaches the ballots, come as no surprise.

Given that the LGBT movement is just over fifty years old and that we face adversaries who claim to represent Christianity's two thousand years of traditional theology, margins of defeat on the order of 70 percent against us and 30 percent for us seem less defeats in fair fights and more the pummeling of vulnerable people by bullies. Although Christianity is not the state religion in the United States and we are not a "Christian nation," the majority of people who worship regularly do so in Christian or Catholic churches. Politicians and other opinion leaders evince wariness about criticizing the churches, because they command such large and loyal followings and can mobilize massive public outcries against commentaries labeled as having an anti-Christian bias.

An Unrelenting Enemy with Powerful Friends

In the days following the 2004 presidential election, James Dobson delivered an unequivocal message. On November 12, 2004, *Slate* magazine published a story by Michael Crowley about Dobson's powerful role in politics as "The Religious Right's New Kingmaker." It included this account of Dobson's postelection message to the White House: "He's already leveraging his new power. When a thank-you call came from the White House, Dobson issued the staffer a blunt warning that Bush 'needs to be more aggressive' about pressing the religious right's pro-life, anti-gay rights agenda, or it would 'pay a price in four years.' "

There is no shortage of lower-level politicians who adhere to Dobson's right-wing social agenda and especially his hostility toward civil rights for LGBT people. On August 24, 2006, the California State Assembly debated a bill that would permit same-sex couples to file joint state tax returns, which later was passed by both the California Assembly and the Senate. As reported by the *Advocate* on August 24, 2006, Republican assemblyman Dennis Mountjoy of Monrovia spoke in opposition to the proposal, saying, "What you seek in society is acceptance. But your lifestyle is abnormal. It is abnormal. It is sexually deviant behavior." On the very same day, U.S. congresswoman Katherine Harris of Florida told the *Florida Baptist Witness*, "Civil rights have to do with individual rights and I don't think they apply to gay issues. I have not supported gay marriage and I do not support any civil rights actions with regard to homosexuality."

Allies in the Pulpits and the Pews

Even as the Antigay Industry grinds on, LGBT people have friends and allies in religious communities. Denominations that have fully committed to the LGBT equality agenda include the United Church of Christ and the Unitarian Universalist Association. Many congregations, or "meetings," of the Society of Friends, commonly known as Quakers, have long welcomed LGBT members and support a broad range of LGBT rights. The Metropolitan Community Church and the Unity Fellowship Church were both formed by LGBT people seeking a safe home in which to come together as Christians. These religious groups represent about 2 million members, a very small fraction of the population. The power of their support lies not in their relative small size, though, but rather in the willingness of leaders and members to actively support LGBT rights in political spheres. The United Church of Christ, the Unitarian Universalist Association, and the American Friends Service

Committee all have long-established and funded LGBT activist programs both within and outside the denominations.

In other larger denominations, LGBT issues regularly incite conflict and provoke debates over church doctrine and practices. These ongoing debates bring LGBT people and issues into the spotlight, giving opportunity to LGBT advocates and allies to press for positive change. The denominational struggles over homosexuality, while internal and often theological in nature, bring LGBT issues to a very large and attentive audience. High-profile struggles over church doctrines about homosexuality are ongoing within the Presbyterian Church USA, the Episcopal Church in the United States, the United Methodist Church, and the Evangelical Lutheran Church in America, with combined memberships of nearly 20 million. The doctrinal conflicts about ordaining LGBT people as ministers and blessing same-sex unions are unresolved, but the ongoing struggles signal hope for change and are an important way to engage church people and bring more to our side.

Organizing work goes on at the congregational level too. The Institute for Welcoming Resources, a project to support pro-LGBT organizing in mainline Protestant and Unitarian churches, counts nearly twenty-five hundred congregations nationwide that have opened their doors to welcome LGBT people and have pledged to support LGBT equality initiatives. These congregations, in a way similar to municipal governments, comprise a fertile foundational site of pro-LGBT organizing, from which positive change can filter up to the higher organizational levels of their denominations.

The Christian denominations mentioned here differ on their national organizational commitment to LGBT issues, but within each denomination can be found ministers, lay leaders, and congregants who have spoken out consistently in support of LGBT people. They build a bulwark against the unrelenting condemnations of homosexuality coming from fundamentalist Christian leaders. Our religious allies effectively and passionately deliver a message of God's love for LGBT people.

Jews for Gays

This discussion of LGBT allies within communities of faith has focused on Christian allies and LGBT organizing within Christian contexts. But we can't overlook the significant support that comes from Jewish communities, congregations, and organizations. Coming from a particular history and understanding of oppression and a tradition of social action, Jewish activists have taken strong leadership roles in many social justice movements, including the black civil rights struggle and antiwar movements. Jews in the United States comprise slightly less than 3 percent of the population, but often make up 4 to 5 percent of voters, depending on the elections. Jewish voters, in significant majorities, support Democratic presidential candidates. For example, Jewish voters supported John Kerry for president in 2004 with 76 percent of their votes.

Jewish organizations, both synagogues and community-based secular groups, express wide-ranging political views, from very progressive to very conservative. Observing Jews attend synagogues that align with four major branches or movements in the United States: Orthodox, Conservative, Reform, and Reconstructionist. The Orthodox movement rejects homosexual behavior as forbidden by their interpretation of Jewish law and does not ordain openly LGBT people. The Reform and Reconstructionist movements ordain openly LGBT people as rabbis and consistently take pro-LGBT positions on political issues and call for the blessings of same-sex unions in their religious practice. The Religious Action Center lobbies in Washington on a full political agenda, including LGBT rights, endorsed by Reform congregations and rabbis. The United Synagogue of Conservative Judaism, representing 760 synagogues, opposed the Federal Marriage Amendment, but has not yet fully resolved the question of ordaining openly LGBT people as rabbis. As we seek alliances with communities of faith, reaching out to Jewish organizations and synagogues, through national and local networks, will bring us into contact with pockets of strong support.

Into the Maw of the Antigay Industry

Faced with such a formidable foe and one that wields its power at the highest levels of government, we might conclude that there is simply no way to win. But the Christian right-wing anti-LGBT movement only *seems* unbeatable. We take inspiration in knowing that the LGBT movement, much smaller but propelled by ideals of freedom and equality, can claim significant gains. As of 2005, about 50 percent of American residents live in a city, county, or state that bans discrimination on the basis of sexual orientation; 27 percent live in jurisdictions that ban discrimination on the basis of gender identity or expression. We achieved this by doing the hard and necessary grunt work of community and political organizing; in fact, it's the only way that we achieve any of our goals. So let's get to it by employing strategies that are effective in challenging our Christian right-wing opponents.

When They Lie, We Reply

As activists and LGBT Americans, we must never permit a right-wing defamation to go unanswered. In public debate, often but not always conducted through media outlets, the most harmful response to a right-wing attack on our human dignity is silence. When we hear a statement that impugns our humanity, our morality, our right to exist, we can respond with a true and accurate testimony refuting the attack. Organizers fighting the 1978 Briggs Initiative, which would have prohibited LGBT people from teaching in public schools, honed this tactic by holding town hall meetings and community forums across California. After stinging defeats in Anita Bryant's campaigns in Florida, Wichita Kansas, St. Paul, Minnesota, and Eugene, Oregon, the tactic of coming out publicly against the homophobic Briggs Initiative, in both small towns and large cities, was successfully used to defeat Briggs and to halt that decade's anti-LGBT campaigns.

Some venues for speaking out about LGBT issues include letters to

the editor of a newspaper, recorded response lines for radio and electronic media, speaking at a public forum or meeting or legislative hearing or in the classroom, phoning in to radio talk shows, writing our own
opinion pieces for print media, or participating in public demonstrations. When our right-wing adversaries speak into a void, listeners and
readers are left on their own to assess the truth of the charge, often re-
lying on their own unexamined prejudices against homosexuality.

During the 2004 public debates in Massachusetts about same-sex
marriage, LGBT activists learned that the four Catholic bishops of
Massachusetts asked all the priests in the state to read letters aloud at
Mass the week before the legislature was scheduled to vote to strip
away the right to marry. The bishops' letter appealed to parishioners to
contact their legislators, urging them to vote in favor of the constitutional amendment to ban same-sex marriage. As a lesbian and a former
Catholic, I could not allow this letter to be delivered at my neighborhood church without any response. After all, the good people who gathered at the Blessed Sacrament Church every Sunday across the street
from my home lived on my street. I attended Mass on Sunday morning,
February 8, 2004. After the priest read the letter, I stood up in the pew
and said, "Forgive me, Father, I have sinned many times since my last
Confession thirty-five years ago. I live across the street with my partner and our two children. Our kids attend public school with some of
the children of this parish. I want you to know that my family wishes
no harm to your families. I ask that you respect our family as we respect yours. Please do not support the Constitutional Amendment that
would exclude our family from the protections and responsibilities
granted through marriage. We only want to take care of each other in
the best way we can, just as you do. Thank you and God bless."

Not all of us would feel able to interrupt the presiding priest at a
Catholic Mass. But each of us can respond to attacks in ways that are
most comfortable for us. For some, holding a sign or banner at a public demonstration to express our support for LGBT rights provides a
comfortable opportunity to refute right-wing defamations or call attention to an instance of anti-LGBT bigotry. In 1999, during Creating

Change, the annual LGBT political conference held in Oakland, California, that year, a young transwoman had been attacked on the street and lay bleeding from lacerations. A police officer who was called to help her instead verbally abused her, saying that she was trash that ought not to be on the streets. Working at lightning speed, organizers planned a demonstration to march from the conference site to the Oakland Police Department. The demonstration prompted an apology from the commanding officer and resulted in establishment of a police liaison to the LGBT community of Oakland. The demonstration was important for LGBT people in Oakland and meaningful for those who marched. But for others, a letter to the editor or a private letter to a public official works best. We begin where and when we can, but we hold up our heads and our humanity with pride and dignity and we do not let verbal attacks go unanswered.

Speak to the Broader Audience

Although I directly addressed the priest at Blessed Sacrament Church, I really spoke to the people in the pews, my neighbors. I spoke to them as someone who shares a street, a neighborhood, a playground, a public school, and the counter at the corner store. In my brief remarks, I asked for their respect of my family and I presented myself as a refutation to the charge that same-sex marriage would harm their families. My neighbors—our neighbors—are not bad or hateful people because they worship at a church that disseminates anti-LGBT sentiment, a view with which they may not agree. Assume the goodness of others; assume their interest in other people; assume their capacity to be open to ideas that are different from what they are told by their ministers or their political leaders.

We sometimes deal with decision makers who don't know much about our lives, in secular as well as religious contexts. In seeking gender-neutral restrooms on campuses, for example, meeting face-to-face with administrators and sharing our own experiences of discomfort, and sometimes actual danger, in using sex-specific facilities can be very compelling. Present the real-life evidence to support administrators in their decisions to change the everyday experiences of transgender and gender-variant people on campus. Be willing to enlighten people to what it means to live as transgender persons in a culture that knows little about us.

When we engage in public discussions at meetings or in legislative hearings, we may be tempted to respond to anti-LGBT defamations with vitriol or condemnations that equal those coming from our detractors. After all, it is frustrating to listen to lies and distortions without being tempted to seek emotional satisfaction by responding to their fiery rhetoric with our own fiery rhetoric. But it is not to those who defame us that we speak; it is the other listeners who need to hear our words, delivered in a way that invites them to listen actively and carefully. Drawing potential supporters into the ongoing rhetorical battle between us and our adversaries will only alienate the undecided. With firmness and calmness, with a steady and tempered voice, we can make our claim for equality, for fairness, for respect in order to win the support of people who have not yet decided where they stand and remain open to hearing about our lives, or have never been encouraged to examine their own prejudices and lack of knowledge.

Biblically Challenged? Don't Argue Chapter and Verse!

When the anti-LGBT leaders use biblical verse and text against us, it is almost irresistible to engage them in spirited exchange. But we all do best sticking to what we know, so let the biblically informed make the biblical arguments. If we are members of a community of faith, we do well to draw on that experience and to stand on that ground, identifying ourselves as believers and followers of that faith.

Christian fundamentalists support their anti-LGBT rhetoric by citing a handful of biblical texts the meanings of which are subjects of great dispute and disagreement among biblical scholars. U.S. Christian fundamentalists hew to a literal interpretation of these few chosen texts, but those interpretations are far from universally accepted. Further, the Bible is replete with proscriptions on behavior that have long since fallen by the wayside. For example, Old Testament biblical codes of conduct prohibit eating pork or shellfish, marking the body with tattoos, touching pigskin, wearing blended fabrics, mixing different seeds during planting, and sexual relations between a husband and wife if the woman is menstruating. The laser-like focus of Christian fundamentalists on a few chosen and disputed texts used to condemn homosexuality amounts to extremely selective application of biblical codes. But we will be wiser to avoid arguing our points on their ground. It leads us into a never-ending and circular debate over interpretations of Scripture and the authority of the Bible. We fare better when we simply point out that, in this country, we abide by separation of church and state; the laws of states and the nation are founded on principles of equality, freedom, self-determination, and tolerance for different religious views, but no religion can determine the laws under which we all live.

Work In and With Communities of Faith

The pews in even the most intractably homophobic churches hold dissenters, even if that dissent remains unspoken. But some people of faith who have dissented from their denomination's historically negative positions on homosexuality have successfully organized to make profound changes within their churches, transforming God from a weapon against us to an ally in our struggle. While this kind of organizing may seem far removed from concerns with civil law and policies, the pro-LGBT movement created within faith communities has far-reaching implications. The LGBT-supportive denominations and congregations typically encourage members to take action on political issues, much like the Christian fundamentalist churches do. These pro-LGBT advocates from faith communities constitute an important countermovement and present theological alternatives to anti-LGBT religious arguments, neutralizing fundamentalists' assertions that only their views can be theologically correct. In the United States, we subscribe to a foundational principle that state and church remain separated, but that does not exclude any of us, as engaged citizens, from participating in civic affairs and democratic processes.

Communities of faith are membership organizations and are responsive to the needs, concerns, and new ideas of members. As *members* of congregations, temples, worship circles of all kinds, we can instigate organizing to move our home congregation in a more LGBT-positive direction. But, first, ask about the congregation's history and its current positions about homosexuality. We may be pleasantly surprised by finding much of what we want is already in place. If we discover that our congregation has done little about LGBT issues, get started. Whether on campus or in the community, we can launch and lead a study group to learn about our faith's views on social issues like homosexuality and to understand better the foundations of those views. We can form a social justice or LGBT-specific group, both for personal growth/support and advocacy within the church or temple. Form a committee or working group to consider ways the congregation can be more welcoming to LGBT people. Take that a step further and meet with the congregational leaders, both clerical and lay leaders, to propose specific changes, like becoming a "welcoming congregation." Join the choir and suggest songs and music with social justice themes and content. Consider becoming part of the lay leadership team at the church. Take on responsibility for the overall well-being of the temple, getting to know others who contribute and care about its community and becoming more a part of that.

For those of us who do not belong to any church, temple or worship circle, we can still build relationships with pro-LGBT congregations to work with them outside their congregations. Learn what churches and temples in your community already support LGBT rights. When forming coalitions to work on specific projects, reach out to them and invite them to send a representative. Ask faith leaders to sign on to petitions and statements of support, and to write letters to the editor. Form an interfaith committee to bring together faith leaders from many traditions to work together. When a crisis erupts on campus or in your community, ask trusted faith leaders for help; crisis counseling and crisis management are occupational fortes of ministers and rabbis. Ask supportive faith leaders to have direct contact with politicians and community leaders to build support for your project. Ministers, rabbis and other clerical leaders have special and respected status in most communities. Call on clerical allies to talk to secular leaders, who often give special consideration to the views of religious leaders.

Be Informed about the Range of Religious Thinking on the Issues

We live in a religious society, one in which most people declare themselves members of a religious denomination or group or say they believe in a deity. Religious organizations cover a broad swath of ideological territory and hold opinions on all aspects of life in the United States, from peace and war to child-rearing to taxes to evolution to social issues like sexuality, homosexuality, and gender variance in humans. If we are not involved in a religious practice, we are less likely to tune in to the commentaries coming from religious quarters, but because so many of our neighbors do, we should pay attention. The Religious Institute on Sexual Morality, Justice, and Healing is an excellent source of the newest thinking about sexuality issues among religious leaders. Other sources about sexuality, sex education and reproductive rights from a religious perspective include Catholics for a Free Choice and the Religious Coalition for Reproductive Choice. Religious thinking on sexuality is anything but monolithic.

GAME PLAN FOR CHAPTER SIX
Anti-LGBT Organizations

Although there remain some pockets of secular opposition to LGBT equality and social justice, the overwhelming majority of organizations currently working against us are religious in outlook, membership, and leadership. Our most entrenched and determined adversaries derive their anti-LGBT positions from their interpretations of religious texts like the Bible and frame their attacks with religious words of condemnation. As disheartening as it sometimes can be to learn more about these groups, it is useful to develop a deeper awareness of their goals, their rhetoric, and their ways of mobilizing their members to act against us in political contexts. Go right to the source by typing some key phrases into your search engine: traditional family values organizations, or the names of any of the anti-LGBT groups mentioned in this chapter. The National Association for Research and Therapy of Homosexuality is an organization of anti-LGBT fringe social scientists that promotes the "curing" of homosexuality. One organization that requires a different key phrase is the Westboro Baptist Church of Topeka, Kansas, the developers of the very vicious Web site and catchphrase "God hates fags." Go there for a sampling of the unvarnished views of determined homophobes.

Try This at Home: Organize against the "Ex-Gay" Movement

The national anti-LGBT organization Focus on the Family convenes conferences to promote the idea that sexual orientation and gender identity can be changed. These so-called "conversion therapy" meetings disseminate anti-LGBT political rhetoric and fuse that with evangelical Christian methods of witnessing and ministering to LGBT people in an effort to convert us to heterosexuality, rigid conformity with traditional roles for men and women, and living what they define as a good Christian life. Mix in a healthy dose of pseudoscience about formations of LGBT identities and you get an indoctrination session into the "ex-gay" movement, which preaches and advocates that, with the right amount of personal willpower and help from God, LGBTs can give up lives of sin. Since 1998, Focus on the Family has organized thirty-six of these conferences under the name "Love Won Out," and although these events are the largest and most well-known of the "ex-gay" movement, other right-wing Christian groups peddle their own brands of conversion ministries and their own lists of former homosexuals who can testify to their personal transformations to heterosexuality.

LGBT activists and organizers may be tempted to regard the "ex-gay" conferences as purely political events hosted by opponents of our political goals. Though anti-LGBT politics is a prime motivator of the organizers of "ex-gay" conferences and meetings, they also operate under the rubric of religion and religious belief. These events occur in the context of freedoms of religion, speech, and assembly, rights that are precious to us, too. We need, also, a response that takes into account a broad public understanding that the religious convictions of American Christians must be respected and that there can be differing and even equally legitimate views about what "causes" homosexuality and gender variance. With these complications in mind, there are two responses to when an "ex-gay" conference comes to town, both of which challenge the assumptions and stereotypes being promulgated by the "ex-gay" organizers.

Although the organizing suggestions that follow are designed specifically to respond to "ex-gay" conferences, they can be tailored for use when other religiously based anti-LGBT events occur in your community.

Hold an interfaith service to celebrate sexual/gender diversity and to heal and repair the social wound of homophobia. By working together with leaders of LGBT-friendly congregations and faiths, we challenge the notion that the problem is our sexuality and gender identity by identifying the problems of homophobia and gender rigidity. The service will be best planned for the same day or weekend of the "ex-gay" conference and, if possible, at a nearby place of worship to the conference location. Including short sermons from several different clerical leaders demonstrates that there is no religious unanimity about LGBT people and identities. Planning a service that includes music, some personal testimonies from LGBT people, and a blessing of those gathered together provides LGBT people who feel personally hurt and offended by the "ex-gay" event the opportunity to be in a supportive and loving environment, sheltered from the homophobia inherent in the notion that our LGBT identities are fundamentally wrong and must be changed. Reaching out to supportive congregations builds good will between and among faith leaders and LGBT organizers, increasing prospects for productive collaboration in the future. Most importantly, we are calling on our supportive faith leaders to help us in a time of trouble and attack on our community.

Organize a press conference or mini-conference to debunk the "ex-gay" event. Because a significant portion of the "ex-gay" ideology rests on the presentation of pseudo-scientific theories about sexuality and gender formation and suggests that homosexuality is a problem to be solved, an "ex-gay" event presents the opportunity to present the views of established sciences of psychology, medicine, and sociology. The "ex-gay" evidence of a connection between pedophilia and homosexuality and claims that homosexuality is shaped by bad relationships between parents and children or by sexual abuse of children and claims that children of LGBT parents suffer psychological damage in their families all deserve strong and public refutation. Begin this organizing by contacting the state affiliates of professional organizations that represent reputable practitioners: the American Psychological Association, the American Academy of Pediatrics, the National Association of Social Workers. These groups can direct you to academic and professional experts who will be able to present research data on homosexuality and LGBT families. Invite the professional organizations to co-sponsor the event with your organization. Call the press conference, or mini-conference, on the same day or same weekend as the "ex-gay" event.

Contact the media to ensure coverage. Media outlets will doubtless be contacted by the "ex-gay" organizers and should be advised of your counterevent. While these types of events may not feel as cathartic or satisfying as a rambunctious demonstration on the street outside the "ex-gay" conference, each makes important critiques of the basic tenets of the "ex-gay" movement: that LGBT people are immoral sinners who need to be saved and that LGBT identities need to be cured to rid society of the problem of homosexuality. Just as important, these events allow LGBT activists to call on allies to advocate on our behalf, belying the notion that we stand alone.

7

Sex, Sex, Always Sex

From the first glimmers of LGBT community organizing in the 1950s to the present-day political struggles over same-sex marriage and other LGBT issues, our opponents have exploited a generalized popular ignorance of and revulsion to homosexual activity. Irrespective of the particular issue, LGBT people are demonized as a threat to social coherence and stability because we pursue our erotic attraction to persons of the same sex. This vilification comes with dire warnings of our corrosive impact on heterosexuality as represented by the "traditional family," regarded by our most hard-line adversaries as the very foundation of society.

This view of homosexuals as subversive agents appears repeatedly throughout the history of the LGBT project to claim homosexuality as equally as "good" as heterosexuality. For example, openly homosexual government workers, or workers even suspected of being homosexual, were targeted by anti-Communist zealots in postwar 1950s America. Because a few spectacular spy cases concerning intelligence material delivered to agents of the then Soviet Union involved federal employees who were suspected of being gay, all known or assumed homosexual government workers were also assumed to be potential Soviet spies. Openly gay men and closeted gay men lost their jobs in the anti-Communist fervor of the Cold War, almost none of whom had ever plotted to betray their government. Historians estimate that thousands of men lost government jobs during the 1950s witch hunts. But a worker's performance or the value of his service never mattered in these cases. The charge of homosexuality inevitably drew the inference of disloyalty. In describing the arc of this smear, Mattachine Society founder Harry Hay recalled, in a September 1999 interview in the *Progressive*, "'Pinko-commie-queer'—that was the thing you heard all over the place."

From Witch Hunts to Military Discharges

The government's 1950s witch hunts against openly homosexual people or those suspected of being homosexual in government service jobs lives on in the U.S. military's policy to discharge openly lesbian, gay, and bisexual servicemembers. The policy, called "Don't Ask, Don't Tell" (DADT), states: "A basis for discharge exists if . . . the member has said that he or she is a homosexual or bisexual, or made some other statement that indicates a propensity or intent to engage in homosexual acts." While the DADT policy improved the previous practices of using military investigative agencies to ferret out lesbian, gay, or bisexual servicemembers for discharge, this is the only law in the United States that *requires* the dismissal from employment of a person who identifies as lesbian, gay, or bisexual. Since the Don't Ask, Don't Tell policy went into effect in 1994, eleven thousand members of all military branches have been discharged for voluntarily disclosing their sexual orientation. Only an act of Congress can rewrite the military policy to discharge openly LGB servicemembers, which cost taxpayers an estimated $364 million over the policy's first decade, according to a February 2006 report, *Financial Analysis of Don't Ask, Don't Tell: How Much Does the Gay Ban Cost?* by the Center for the Study of Sexual Minorities in the Military at the University of California at Santa Barbara.

Charles Moskos, a sociology professor at Northwestern University and one of the policy's architects, argued (as reported by Josh White in the *Washington Post*, " 'Don't Ask' Costs More Than Expected," February 14, 2006) that the policy should be retained because heterosexual servicemembers would be uncomfortable living in close quarters with gay servicemembers, an argument that echoes the military's long-standing resistance to racial integration that was advocated by civil rights groups following World War II, when the federal government continued to argue that white soldiers would be uncomfortable sharing living quarters with black soldiers. During the 1993 debates over lesbian, gay, and bisexual inclusion in the armed forces, Georgia Democratic senator Sam Nunn, chair of the Senate Armed Services Committee, famously, and in front of television cameras, inspected the berthing quarters on a naval ship to illustrate just how closely shipmates lived. Nunn inferred that it would be dangerous for straight naval personnel to share sleeping quarters with gay sailors.

Nunn's exploitation of heterosexual anxiety over homosexuality won the day. President Bill Clinton's efforts to dispense entirely with the military's policies of discrimination against lesbian, gay, and bisexual soldiers and sailors was spectacularly defeated, leaving Don't Ask, Don't Tell as a compromise that supports the implication that identified homosexuals are categorically untrustworthy with the defense of the country. The current version of military discrimination enforces the idea that LGB servicemembers must, for the sake of the military's mission, live closeted and secret lives. Ironically, forty years earlier, homosexual "secrecy" was the government's primary rationale for firing qualified, capable, and loyal homosexual government employees. If their homosexuality became known to foreign agents, they were said to be vulnerable to blackmail, trading government secrets to protect their own secret of homosexuality. Don't Ask, Don't Tell turns that notion on its head and concludes that it is announced homosexuality that threatens the country, and that the closet is the proper place for LGB servicemembers.

Homosexual = Untrustworthy?

No matter which way LGBT people turn, our sexuality is our Achilles' heel: if we are open about it in the military, we destroy unit cohesion; if we are secret about it, we might betray the country. Either way, we can't be trusted, and that is the completely irrational point. The reality is that social scientists estimate that sixty-five thousand LGB servicemembers are in the armed forces, without apparent harm to the military mission (see Gary Gates, *Gay Men and Lesbians in the U.S. Military: Estimates from Census 2000*, Urban Institute, 2004). Our opponents claim that gay marriages will destroy straight marriages, but the reality is that eight thousand legally married same-sex couples in Massachusetts have not harmed the other 60 million or so intact marriages in the United States.

Clearly, logic and rational thinking play no role in these homophobic arguments. What is it about same-sex orientation and behavior that is so threatening to our opponents? Our adversaries on the Religious Right say that God opposes homosexuality and so they must oppose it, too. Other arguments include:

- Homosexuality is not natural (by which they mean that homosexuality is not procreative).
- Homosexuality is not a social and cultural norm.
- Homosexuality deprives children of a mother or a father.
- Approval of homosexuality marks the decline of civilization.
- Homosexual relationships are unstable, and this instability will be transmitted to stable family units.
- Homosexuality represents the slippery slope toward the acceptance of other perversions: incest, bestiality, and polygamy.

All these arguments can be condensed to: homosexual behavior is immoral, therefore homosexual people are immoral, therefore homosexual people are undeserving of full citizenship and participation in civic and community life. The more we insist on legitimizing our sexuality by establishing our legal equality, the more fervid our opponents become.

Claiming Our Morality

In order to counter the right wing's claim of the immorality of same-sex sexuality, we must articulate the following counterstatements:

- Sexual orientation is morally neutral.
- Neither heterosexuality nor homosexuality nor bisexuality, by itself, is morally good or morally bad.

- Sexuality exists within people to be experienced with others.
- Sexual orientation is not morally valued in our laws or Constitution.
- Human beings, no matter their sexual orientation, live their lives in moral or immoral ways by how they conduct their relationships and how they treat other people, other creatures, and the environment.
- LGBT people agree to be judged by how we treat others, but we refuse to be condemned on account of our sexuality.

Same-sex relationships, just like opposite-sex relationships, contribute to the well-being of human beings. To deny LGBT people basic needs like housing and employment, dignity, and unfettered access to human connection, closeness, and intimacy is to deny us our birthright as human beings. Heterosexual people can no longer claim closeness and connection as their special privilege by denigrating our relationships and families or by denying us the same legal protections afforded them. We, too, care for each other, sometimes over a lifetime, and that is valuable, to us, to our families, and to the larger family of humanity.

Sexual pleasure is a positive and fulfilling experience for humans, whether in the context of long-term relationships, short affairs, or fleeting encounters. When our lives are bereft of sexual pleasure, we mourn for it and try to find ways to experience it. One of the great gifts that LGBT people can share with others is the ennobling aspect of sexual pleasure for its own sake, without shame or fear or apprehension. Uncoupled from the potential for reproduction and its accompanying anxieties, same-sex pleasure stands as a wonderful example to others that the joys of sexual and reciprocal gratification can soothe and comfort us and assuage feelings of isolation.

LGBT people form families for the same reasons straight people do: to care for those we love and to be cared for in return. Families in LGBT communities include couples in long-term sexual relationships, with or without children, domestic partnerships not defined by a sexual relationship between partners, familial households of committed adults, and caring relationships among networks of friends who do not share living spaces or a household. These family formations are healthful and affirming ways to provide their members with love and support.

Families formed by LGBT people pose a constructive challenge to male supremacy and patriarchy. When we join together to create family, in whatever form we choose, we enter into that project without preordained notions of how the tasks and work of family life will be assigned. Two women together or two men together or a household of adults must devise for themselves a domestic work plan that does not rely on the rigid gender roles of the traditional ideas of men's work and women's work. Household tasks are divvied up depending on skills, interests, and availability of the partners. In a 1950s-style fantasy family, father dominated mother and children and worked outside the home, providing an income on which all others relied. Mother procreated and raised the children, tending to the daily household tasks rather than her own career interests. When there is no father/mother combination, the partners necessarily take up work that would have been proscribed under traditional notions of gender. LGBT patterns of family life concretely give shape to a goal of the modern feminist movement: that the work required to manage a household be shared by its members without regard to their genders. Further, LGBT people transmit to others around them the understanding that there is no such thing as "women's work" or "men's work" and that equal work for equal people works.

We want to live in families, communities, and a country that values LGBT people enough to let us survive, thrive, and contribute to the common good. Discrimination against us denies us social safety and limits our opportunities to participate in all spheres of life, and that is immoral and unacceptable.

"No Homo" Zones

Full integration of LGB people into military service and access to marriage are the two contemporary lightning rod issues for our movement, in part because these two institutions have been protected as "no homo" zones. Our adversaries see defending the military and marriage from the contamination of homosexuality as their last stand against what they see as our perversity and immorality. When Don't Ask, Don't Tell falls, as it inevitably will, openly LGB people will serve in the armed forces, raising the social contradictions of discrimination against us in civilian life. In the states where we cannot now be married or where we are not protected from arbitrary discrimination in the workplace, LGBT people live under a two-tiered regime of citizenship: categorically denied access to legal protections that remain categorically available to heterosexuals.

But there are other no-homo zones that become sites of public debate and controversy, inciting our opponents to label homosexuality as destructive and immoral. The visibility of openly LGBT teachers in schools and the inclusion of LGBT-related material in classrooms and curricula routinely prompts a backlash. Opposition to forming gay-straight alliances in high schools often revolves around the charge that these student clubs are recruiting tools for the LGBT movement and will cause students to experiment with being gay and entering into a destructive "lifestyle." Demands for full inclusion of LGBT history in classes and textbooks bring charges that teaching students about the substantive contributions of LGBT people to public life will honor immoral behavior. Gender-neutral restrooms are said to cause confusion about the centrality and unquestionable rightness of two unambiguous genders. Teachers who come out or undertake a gender transition on the job are accused of being bad role models for their students, causing them to question a naturalness of biological sex as the determinant of gender.

The Boy Scouts of America, deemed a private organization by the courts despite its utilization of publicly owned facilities, maintains a strict policy of denying membership to gay, bisexual, or transgender youth and denying leadership positions to openly gay, bisexual, or transgender men. Predicated on their belief that homosexuality is immoral, the Boy Scouts won their case, *Boy Scouts v. Dale*, at the U.S.

Supreme Court in 2000 when the Court agreed that the Boy Scouts could restrict membership based on their freedom of association. Similarly, the Ancient Order of Hibernians coordinates the annual Saint Patrick's Day parade in New York City, the largest event of its kind in the country, and does not permit LGBT organizations to participate. This group, like the Boy Scouts considered a private organization, is permitted to exclude LGBT groups even though the parade is held on public streets and utilizes public services each year. The Supreme Court ruled in its favor in 1995 in *Hurley vs. GLIB*. Some analysts interpret these two Court rulings not as losses for the LGBT community, but rather as affirmations of the right of organizers to control who may associate and participate in events and groups they coordinate and control. While there are differences of opinion about the broad impact of these decisions, the Boy Scouts and New York's Saint Patrick's Day parade remain public spaces in which LGBT participation and visibility is categorically denied.

From the insult of being barred from an ethnic cultural celebration of Saint Patrick's Day to the discernible and daily damages that result from erasure in schools and classrooms and the dangers of sex-segregated restrooms, LGBT people endure exclusions that emanate from the moral condemnations that we must resist and refute.

Taking It to the People

Some LGBT activists feel discomfited and troubled at the prospect of claiming sexual pleasure and LGBT sexuality and gender expression as moral positives. After all, by proclaiming the moral goodness of gayness, won't we pick a fight with our opponents? Wouldn't it be easier to avoid the discussion of sex altogether? The reality is that our opponents condemn our sexuality, and, more recently, nonconforming gender expression, whether or not we raise the topic. We have been shunned, demeaned, derogated, defamed, beaten, killed, and denied fundamental rights under the law because of our sexuality and gender identifications.

There has been no escaping the oppression of homosexuality and, as important, there is no effective end run around the right wing's persistent attempts to discredit us on account of sexuality. We deny our sexual goodness at great cost to the goals and integrity of our social-change movement and at great cost to our own humanity. The moral discussion of sexuality is very much a public concern and when we try to wish away or avoid that public discussion, we lose the argument before we've entered it.

The necessary public moral discussion about sexuality doesn't contradict the struggle for equality. If we want equality, then we must work for sexual self-determination and freedom. When our opponents demean us by naming our sexual behavior perverted, they aim to discredit our equality claims. They claim that the law doesn't protect sexual perverts, it prosecutes them. Because the LGBT movement has successfully stripped away two of our adversaries' most potent arguments—that we're mentally ill and we're criminals—the only remaining argument they have is the baseless claim that we are an immoral people. At every opportunity, we must refute this last argument against our full participation in society.

Levels of the public's acceptance of homosexuality have changed and increased since the movement's founders began their work in the 1950s. If our families, neighbors, political leaders, and opinion leaders had not become much more accepting, the Christian right-wing anti-LGBT movement would have little reason to complain. Evidence that we have been integrated into popular culture abounds on television and film, in literature and song, and in every kind of media outlet. The love that dared not speak its name now sings, dances, cracks jokes, breaks hearts, solves crimes, heals the sick, and cavorts in cartoon and comic book characterizations. We are everywhere.

The Christian right wing responds to our increasing visibility with sometimes laughable hysteria. Jerry Falwell, the televangelist, declared in 1999 that the children's television character Tinky Winky on *Teletubbies* promoted homosexuality because he or she was purple and carried a pink purse. In 2005 Falwell's colleague James Dobson of Focus on the Family accused the children's television character SpongeBob SquarePants of brainwashing children to be progay, because the character appeared in a video used in a school-based program to promote social tolerance, including tolerance for people of all sexual orientations. But what Falwell and Dobson are really angry about is the presence of real, live-action gay and lesbian characters on television, in films, and in the media. The Christian right-wing leaders vigorously attacked actress and talk show host Ellen DeGeneres's when she came out as a lesbian on *Ellen,* her eponymous television show, in 1997. They were steadfast in denouncing *Will & Grace,* the television show that debuted in 1998 with a gay male lead character, saying that the show normalized the homosexual character Will Truman. Lesbian talk show cohost Rosie O'Donnell raised right-wing Christian hackles in September 2006 when she discussed her coming-out experience and raising children with her lesbian partner on *The View,* a popular daytime women's program.

While positive depictions of LGBT people in popular culture indicate a change in the cultural acceptance of homosexuality, this change is also reflected in the news media's coverage of LGBT issues and people. The coverage of the issue of same-sex marriage has brought unprecedented opportunities to communicate the goodness and value of our lives to millions of Americans. In a sample of editorial opinion dating from August 17, 2005, to August 31, 2006, and gathered by Freedom to Marry and Gay and Lesbian Alliance against Defamation, seventy-eight daily papers ran LGBT-family positive editorials, weighing in on the issue of marriage rights for same-sex couples.

Building Public Consensus

In a fundamental and demonstrable way, we now have broad support in the entertainment industry and the media, as well as support from an increasing number of political leaders. But the facts on the ground in every state where a constitutional amendment to ban same-sex marriage has passed show that, as important as positive media depictions and editorial support can be, we have very far to go with voters and citizens. Our most important task remains unfinished and that is to build a broad public consensus that LGBT people are morally deserving of full citizenship and equality under the law.

The LGBT movement's experience in ballot-initiative campaigns gives a vivid example of how direct communication with people helps our cause. The results of ballot-question campaigns on same-sex marriage are not encouraging: voters in twenty-six states have passed constitutional amendments to ban gay marriage, and one state has defeated an anti-same-sex-marriage amendment. So while we may have support from editorial writers and important opinion leaders, we still must make our case directly to voters, who are the people who actually decide to amend their states' constitutions. The most effective way to communicate directly with individuals is to talk with them. Knock on their doors and talk. Call them on the telephone and talk. Interrupt their shopping day and talk. Look them in the eye and talk. Tell them, face to face, why a proposed constitutional amendment hurts our families and ask them to vote against it.

In 1978, California LGBT activists faced an uphill battle to defeat the Briggs Initiative, a proposed law that would ban lesbian and gay teachers from the state's public schools, scheduled to be voted on that November. In September, polling results showed that the Briggs Initiative would easily pass, and that news spurred LGBT organizers into direct action against Briggs. Armed with clipboards and voter lists, they walked through neighborhoods and talked to voters. Especially important in the campaign were the teachers who came out to neighbors, explaining that the proposed law would cause them to lose their jobs and asking for "no" votes on Briggs. Harvey Milk, a gay man newly elected to the San Francisco Board of Supervisors and one of fewer than five openly LGBT elected officials in the country at that time, also took to the road against the proposed law, debating state senator John Briggs, the initiative's sponsor, in cities and towns across the state. On Election Day, the Briggs Initiative went down to defeat, 58 percent to 42 percent; analysts credited the turnaround with the willingness of ordinary LGBT people to talk directly to voters about how the law would harm them.

No matter what particular issue we are working to resolve, no matter who makes the decision about it, we do best when we interact directly with individuals and explain why an issue matters to us and how they can support and help us. We have not done this nearly often enough: say who we are, what we want, and ask for help. It is not the only way to persuade people to our side, but it is the most direct and effective way and it makes us real to others.

Fight for Freedom; Organize for Equality

Debates within our movement over its priorities, directions, goals, and strategies will continue as long as there is a political movement of LGBT people. Currently, leaders and organizers debate the pace and emphasis of the push for same-sex marriage, which has provoked a strong and sustained backlash against not only same-sex marriage, but also LGBT-positive policies in schools, child adoptions by LGBT people, and recognitions of domestic partnerships. This internal push and pull over strategies and tactics marked our movement's work around AIDS, the military's ban on LGB servicemembers, and the inclusion of transgender issues in our work.

Of critical importance in these strategy debates is that, as organizers, we take the time to reflect on what has gone wrong and what has gone right and what can be done differently in the future. For example, following the enactment of Don't Ask, Don't Tell, some activists observed that collaborating with a newly installed presidential administration to advance so hastily an issue that could only be controversial, without having learned how to work with members of Congress on a less contentious matter, was a massive error of political overreach. President Clinton and the LGBT movement lost confidence and credibility: the president lost confidence on all future issues concerning our communities, and the movement lost credibility because we were unable to quickly mobilize support for the policy change. In 2007 there is a renewed push to lift the military's ban on LGB servicemembers, thirteen years after the establishment of Don't Ask, Don't Tell, and with support of over one hundred members of Congress.

Historically, tensions have also risen over whether we should pursue deeper, more radical change in institutions or seek reform of existing law and policy. Put in a slightly different way, we have debated whether to seek change from outside the political system or become a part of the political system and work from within. The contemporary LGBT movement works within and outside the political system, having both elected LGBT officials and professional advocates/lobbyists moving forward our efforts to reform laws and policies, in addition to energetic organizers who articulate and advocate the newly identified concerns and needs of LGBT people. For example, in the late 1980s when AIDS ravaged gay male communities, organizers with ACT UP targeted the Food and Drug Administration (FDA) in a huge protest action to demand that the agency speed up its process of testing and releasing experimental treatments for AIDS/HIV. Organizers of the mass action, including myself, met with officials at the FDA to tell them in plain language that we intended to occupy the agency and take over their jobs in order to put drugs in the hands of sick people. Demonstrators in the thousands showed up at the agency headquarters the next day and although we failed to take over any FDA employee's job, we shut down the agency. But seeing our determination to seize control of the FDA's operations, agency leaders immediately reached out to a core group of professional health care and drug-access advocates to plan an accelerated process of drug testing. The thousands of demonstrators caught the attention of agency officials in a way that the professional advocates had been unable to do, opening a door for the kind of detailed and scientific discussions that only professional advocates could have with FDA decision makers.

Most important for the success of our political movement is to realize that we work inside and outside the political system, creating pressure for change from the outside and working to achieve change from the inside. We need to maintain respect for the choices of our colleagues about how to address an issue and we need to coordinate our actions so that we can work in tandem toward the same goal. When stubborn decision makers come to understand that they can no longer resist the pressure to change a policy, such as happened within the FDA, we need to be able and willing to articulate in concrete terms what it is we want. The same is true with respect to the merely uninformed administrators on campuses: first we identify a problem and educate them about how we are affected by it, and then we tell them how we want the problem to be solved.

We won't win every battle for LGBT people, and sometimes we will need to fight again and again for a particular issue, which can be discouraging. Over time, our persistence helps to convince decision makers that we are committed to improving our lives. A case in point of the necessity to consistently advocate for a specific goal comes from the histories of nondiscrimination laws. In Massachusetts, LGBT people and groups worked for seventeen years to pass the state's civil rights law banning discrimination on the basis of sexual orientation. Currently, advocates plan for a campaign to amend the law to include the category of gender expression. In New York State, it took the concerted efforts of advocates over twenty-nine years to pass the Sexual Orientation Nondiscrimination Act, a law that now needs updating with the inclusion of gender expression. But we fight on, knowing that nondiscrimination law is a concrete goal that will bring relief to LGBT people who endure arbitrary discrimination in the workplace, enabling us to be out on the job and honest with our coworkers without fear of retribution.

The LGBT goals for equality can be supported by any and all who agree that LGBT people should be full participants in society, irrespective of political party affiliation or membership in a community of faith. All LGBT aspirations to be free from institutional and societal expressions of homophobia and bias against nonconforming gender expression deserve the attention and energy of our movement. Every LGBT person's dream of freedom from oppression is noble, honorable, and inspiring. LGBT silence and erasure in the public sphere is coming to an end; homophobia and gender bias in public and private spheres must not be tolerated, promoted, supported, or promulgated by government entities that work for the good of all people. When we come out and talk to those around us in an honest way about our lives, we will win full equality and sexual freedom and self-determination. We will accept nothing less.

GAME PLAN FOR CHAPTER SEVEN
Embracing Our Sexuality

Many LGBT-positive resources about sexuality are available, including Web sites, printed materials, films and videos, stores that specialize in sex-related merchandise, and sexual health and reproductive health organizations. Some organizations that are especially dedicated to sexuality education are the Sexuality Information and Education Council of the United States, the National Sexuality Resource Center, and Planned Parenthood. Resources especially aimed at youth and young people include Advocates for Youth and Scarleteen. These and other sites with useful and nonjudgmental sexuality information and resources can be found by typing "sexuality education" or "sexuality resources" into your search engine. There are two organizations that discuss sexuality from religious viewpoints: the Center for Sexuality and Religion and the Religious Institute on Sexual Morality, Justice and Healing.

Try This at Home: Let's Talk Sex

Within the LGBT communities and across racial, gender, and age and class lines, there is most often a thunderous silence about sex and sexuality. There is no lack of flirtation and sexual interest, but rarely are we invited to have the kinds of community-building discussions that break down myths and stereotypes about how people within our communities who hold different sexual and gender identities actually feel about sex and sexuality.

Why have the conversation? First, if we are going to claim and defend our right to sexuality and sexual self-determination, we need to practice extending those rights to members of our own communities. Second, sexual subcultures like leather and bears, butches and femmes are greatly valued by our colleagues. In the interest of building a truly representative movement and community, we need to appreciate what is important about these sexual subcultures. Third, given that it is our sexualities that are so consistently under attack by the anti-LGBT forces, we should at least know what it is we are defending. Fourth, sharing with each other what is valued and valuable about LGBT sexuality brings us closer together, as human beings and as a movement for freedom and justice. And last but most important, everyone likes to talk about sex!

Put sex on the table. At a meeting of your LGBT group, suggest that your organization launch a series of conversations called "Let's Talk Sex." Form a small committee to organize the conversations. Describe the Let's Talk Sex discussions as entirely voluntary and intended for members of the group who want to explore the meaning and value of sex and sexuality for LGBT people.

Determine the parameters. Have the organizing group set the topic for each gathering and take responsibility for discussion structure and facilitation. To start, plan the Let's Talk Sex discussions for ninety-minute segments.

Set the ground rules. Ground rules are important to create safety in the group, allowing participants to say what's really on their minds. Few of us are totally comfortable talking sex, and a little extra effort to help people feel secure and confident will go a long way. Examples of effective ground rules are:

- All members of the LGBT organization are welcome to participate.
- Let's Talk Sex conversations are confidential. What gets discussed at Let's Talk Sex stays at Let's Talk Sex.
- Please keep comments to "I" statements.
- Participants agree to suspend judgment of others and avoid making judgments about the content of others' comments, either verbally or nonverbally.

- Since the point of Let's Talk Sex is to learn from each other, participants agree to be active in the group. No silent partners!
- Let's Talk Sex is about consensual sexual behavior between partners. It isn't about exploitation of others or using sex as a way to intimidate or shame other people.

Brainstorm topics for discussion. Discussion topics help ground and frame the conversation. Some suggestions:

- When did we first become aware of our sexuality?
- What were some of our first sexual experiences and what did we learn from those?
- What is our sexual orientation? What is our gender identity?
- When do we feel best about sex? What are the ways sex makes us feel good about ourselves and our partners?
- What kind of sexual activities best express who we are and what we want and like?
- What are the sexual minorities within the LGBT community?
- If we are bisexual, have we experienced discrimination within the LGBT community?
- Do we feel that our sexual orientation is respected?
- If we are transgender, have we experienced discrimination within the LGBT community? Do we feel that our gender identity is respected?
- What do we think about leather sexual culture? Bears? Guys who cruise for sex?
- What is our response at a pride event when we see hunky guys gyrating on floats or drag queens in their finest outfits? Are we embarrassed? Thrilled? Want to cover our children's eyes?
- How does our own understanding of masculinity, femininity, and gender variance affect how we think about LGBT sexuality and community?
- Do we identify as femmes? Butches? Is our erotic desire structured in this way?

- What do we want to share about our sexual practices and likes and dislikes?
- If sex is not in the context of a long-term relationship, is it OK? What constitutes immoral or unacceptable sex and sexuality?
- What values and messages about sex did we learn as children? Do we hold them today?
- If the world were truly accepting of LGBT people, how would our erotic lives be different? Our gender identities?
- What is our vision of a world where all of our sexualities and genders are not only tolerated, but valued and accepted? How can we get there?

Collaborate on going forward. After three or four Let's Talk Sex gatherings, group leaders should check in with participants to see if the group wants to keep meeting. If so, participants can be invited to generate some further topics for discussion, or prioritize topics already brainstormed. After the final meeting, participants can jot down their feedback to the group leaders to help guide the planning for future series of Let's Talk Sex.

Acknowledgments

The inspirations and insights that I have enthusiastically absorbed from colleagues over the past three decades inform the thinking and ideas of this volume and come from sources too numerous to name and some too distant to fully recall. The women and men named below have greatly influenced my organizing work and my understandings of social justice and social change and I thank them for being part of my political world.

From the much-missed *Gay Community News*: Richard Burns, Amy Hoffman, Sherri Edwards, Chris Guilfoy, the late Mike Reigle, and the late Eric Rofes.

From the National Gay and Lesbian Task Force: Jeff Levi, Ivy Young, Kevin Berrill, Peri Jude Radecic, Robert Bray, Scot Nakagawa, Karen Bullock-Jordan, Kerry Lobel, John D'Emilio, Sean Cahill, Dave Fleischer, and Amber Hollibaugh.

From the exciting political city of Cambridge, Massachusetts, my friend and comrade Arthur Lipkin, and Robin Shore, Laura Moskowitz, and Mariah Shore.

My gratitude beyond measure goes to Kris Kleindienst, Ruth Eisenberg, and Urvashi Vaid. These three women are woven into the fabric of my life, giving me the strength of their friendships, the challenge of their ideas, and the support I have most needed at times of crucial political and personal choices.

Thanks also to Matt Foreman, Rea Carey, and Sandi Greene, three staff leaders of the National Gay and Lesbian Task Force, which generously gave me a sabbatical from my work to think and write. Special thanks go to the Movement Building team at the National Gay and Lesbian Task Force, each of whom took on portions of my work during the writing of this book: Julie Childs, Russell Roybal, Lisa Weiner-Mahfuz, Artie Bray, Teresa Haynes, and Robin Wood.

When the words did not easily flow, when the dishes piled up, when extra encouragement was needed, I could count on my family to shoulder more responsibilities, filling in the many gaps produced by my time and attention to this project, and to cheer me up and on. Thank you, Jade McGleughlin, Jesse McGleughlin, Max McGleughlin, Ann Holder, and Frances Kunreuther.

I am both glad and grateful that Beacon Press supports Queer Action/Queer Ideas, the series of which this volume is a part. Thanks to Helene Atwan, Beacon's director, managing editor Lisa Sacks, senior editor Gayatri Patnaik, production coordinator Sarah Gillis, and editorial assistant Tracy Ahlquist.

And finally, I am deeply indebted to my friend, comrade, and Queer Action/Queer Ideas editor Michael Bronski, who has given generously of his political wisdom, editorial insights, and profound cultural vision.

I have benefited enormously from all I have learned from the named and unnamed herein, none of whom should be held responsible for errors, miscalculations, or shortcomings of this book.

Index

ACT UP, 79, 81, 149

adoption, 55, 148

advocacy organizations. *See* organizations for LGBT people

Advocates for Youth, 14–15, 16, 151

affirmative action, 95

AFL-CIO, 22

African Americans: as allies of LGBT community, 90, 102–8; attitudes of, on homosexuality and same-sex marriage, 102–8; bias crime against, 94; and black churches, 104–5, 106, 108; church attendance of, 103–4; families of, 104–5; in military, 67, 138; and National Black Justice Coalition, 24, 108; and slavery, 105, 106; voting rights for, 105. *See also* civil rights movement

After the Ball (Kirk and Madsen), 57

AIDS Action, 22

AIDS/HIV: ACLU project on, 108; FDA and treatment for, 149; funding for services and research on, 93, 108, 111; media coverage of, 46, 61–62, 81; organizing focused on, 57, 79, 81, 148; prevention of, 38, 81; and Reagan administration, 36; and religious right-wing movement, 118

AIDS Memorial Quilt, 36

Al-Fatiha Foundation, 94–95

allies of LGBT people: ACLU as, 108–10; African Americans as, 90, 102–8; building durable alliances, 92–97; Chávez as, 100–102; failures in

alliance building, 110–11; and "gay issues" debate, 93–96, 113; gay-straight alliances (GSAs) at schools, 18–21, 78, 83–87, 143; guidelines on, 111–13; importance of, 90–91; Japanese American Citizens League (JACL) as, 97–100, 101, 111; and LGBT organizers of color, 92–93; in religious communities, 123–25; and social justice/action study group, 114–16; straight elected officials as, 73; three R's of relationships among, 91–92; and unlearning prejudices, 96–97, 114

American Academy of Pediatrics, 135

American Civil Liberties Union (ACLU), 35, 96, 108–10; Lesbian & Gay Rights Project, 22

American Family Association, 119

American Friends Service Committee, 96, 123–24

American Law Institute (ALI), 34, 53

American Psychiatric Association (APA), 50–54, 66

American Psychological Association, 135

American Vision, 119

Ancient Order of Hibernians, 144

anti-Communism, 46–48, 50, 61, 137–38

antidiscrimination laws, 31–32, 41, 71–72, 78, 103, 109, 118–19, 126, 150

Antigay Industry, 117–23, 126–30, 133–36, 140, 145–46

antisodomy laws. *See* sodomy laws

education. *See* colleges and universities; high schools; *and headings beginning with* school
education on LGBT people: community educational forums, 80; and teachable moments, 70–71
Eisenhower, Dwight, 48
Elders, Joycelyn, 102
elected officials: local elected officials, 32–33; openly LGBT people as, 73–75, 82, 147, 149; presidential election (2004), 121, 125; and pride events, 69; running for office, 43–44, 67, 73–74, 82; in state government, 33; statistics on, 32; straight allies as, 73; visits to, 41–42, 81
elections. *See* elected officials; politics; voting
Episcopal Church, 124
Equality California, 100, 101
Equality Federation, 23
Evangelical Lutheran Church, 124
"ex-gay" movement, 133–36

face-to-face interactions, 81, 147–48
Falwell, Jerry, 119, 145, 146
families: children of LGBT parents, 22, 55, 127, 135, 146, 148; feminist model of, 142; as formed by LGBT people, 141–42; patriarchal model of, 142. *See also* parents of LGBT people
Family Pride Coalition, 22
Federal Bureau of Investigation (FBI), 47, 48–49
federal government: barring of homosexuals from jobs in, 48, 51, 52; elected officials in, 32; openly LGBT people as congresspeople, 74, 99; and spy cases, 47–48, 137. *See also* Con-

gress, U.S.; *specific laws and court cases; and government agencies*
Federal Marriage Amendment, 103, 120, 125
fellowships, 17, 21–25
Feminist Majority Foundation, 89
films. *See* media
Focus on the Family, 119–20, 133, 145–46
Food and Drug Administration (FDA), 149, 150
Foreman, Matt, 110, 117
Frank, Barney, 74, 99–100
Freedom to Marry, 23, 146
free speech, 62, 109

Gaither, Billy Joe, 70
Gallo boycott, 100
Gates, Gary, 139
Gay & Lesbian Alliance against Defamation (GLAAD), 24, 61–62, 146, 147
Gay & Lesbian Victory Fund, 23
The Gay Agenda, 58–59
Gay and Lesbian Labor Activist Network (GALLAN), 100
Gay and Lesbian Medical Association, 22
Gay Community News, 57
"gay issues" debate, 93–96, 113
Gay, Lesbian & Straight Education Network (GLSEN), 25
Gay Liberation Front, 28
gay liberation movement, 28–29, 51–54. *See also* LGBT movement
gay men. *See* LGBT people
gay pride. *See* pride events
gay rights, 29, 75. *See also* gay liberation movement; LGBT movement
gay-straight alliances (GSAs) at school, 18–21, 78, 83–87, 143